NORTH COAST 500

**Your guide
to Scotland's
greatest road trip**

CONTENTS

Left The Bealach na Bà, the famous zigzagging mountain pass on the west coast

Introduction

When I was offered the chance to write a book on the North Coast 500, I was so excited. Who wouldn't be? This 516-mile (830-km) journey around Scotland's northern Highlands is regarded as one of the UK's best road trips – and it's easy to see why. The route has it all: historic castles, charming fishing villages and inky lochs, as well as a good helping of stunning coastal scenery. Plus, the Scottish Highlands are close to my heart: Inverness, the route's starting point, was once my home, and there's nothing I love more than exploring the region. This was going to be fun.

And it really was. On the trip we strolled along deserted beaches, admired imposing castles and walked along a geological fault line. We got to see a whole host of local wildlife, too – take, for example, the time we hiked out to a headland on the north coast to see resident puffins. After hours of misty rain, and no sign of their brilliantly vibrant beaks, we finally caught sight of them, nesting on the cliffs and gliding through the air. It's one of my favourite memories.

The best thing about the route, though, was the amazing locals that we met along the way, many of whom are passionate about helping their communities and the environment. On the east coast, we spoke to the folks at Glenmorangie whisky distillery, who are working with the Marine Conservation Society to reintroduce oysters to the Dornoch Firth; on the north coast, we met Joanna, the owner of the cosy Store Cafe, who has created a thriving community hub for locals; and on the west coast, we chatted to Ian the fisherman, who takes visitors out to sea alongside his plucky dog Dubh to teach them about sustainable fishing. There were countless more, too, from climate-change-fighting gardeners to organic beer brewers.

With so many amazing people to meet and places to explore, it's best to take your time on the North Coast 500. After all, the point of the route isn't simply to check off the sights and miles, but to engage with the communities, cultures and landscapes found along the way. It's also about slowing down enough to enjoy those unexpected moments that come from being on the road. For us, that was grooving along to 80s tunes as we negotiated winding single-tracks and eating cheese toasties in the car because it was chucking it down outside.

All this and more awaits you on the North Coast 500. So what are you waiting for? Enjoy every minute of your road-tripping adventure.

Clockwise from top left A resident puffin on Dunnet Head; a single-track section of the route near Loch Eriboll; Ian the fisherman; the white sands of Achmelvich Beach

ON THE MAP

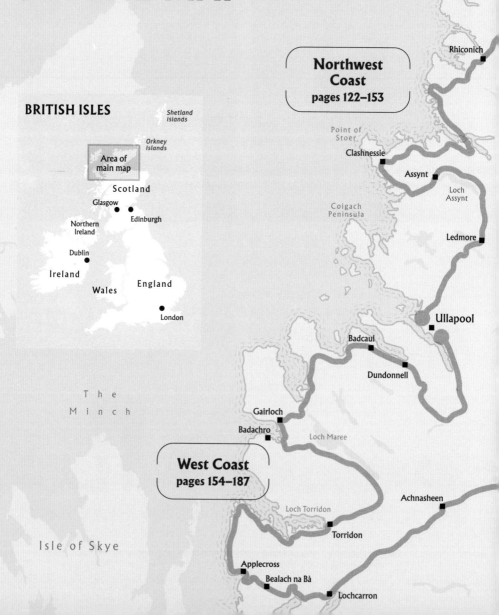

BRITISH ISLES

Shetland Islands

Orkney Islands

Area of main map

Scotland

Glasgow

Edinburgh

Northern Ireland

Dublin

Ireland

Wales

England

London

The Minch

Isle of Skye

Northwest Coast
pages 122–153

Cap Wra

Rhiconich

Point of Stoer

Clashnessie

Assynt

Loch Assynt

Coigach Peninsula

Ledmore

Ullapool

Badcaul

Dundonnell

Gairloch

Badachro

Loch Maree

West Coast
pages 154–187

Achnasheen

Loch Torridon

Torridon

Applecross

Bealach na Bà

Lochcarron

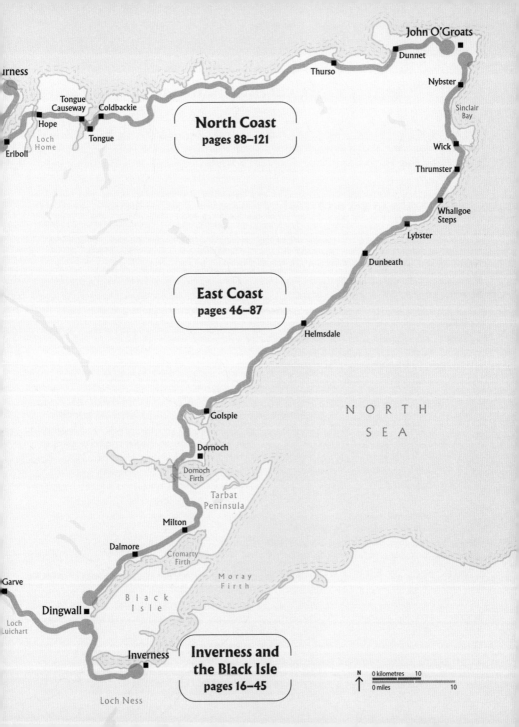

John O'Groats

Dunnet

Thurso

Nybster

Sinclair
Bay

urness

Tongue
Causeway

Coldbackie

Hope

Loch
Home

Tongue

Eriboll

North Coast
pages 88–121

Wick

Thrumster

Whaligoe
Steps

Lybster

Dunbeath

East Coast
pages 46–87

Helmsdale

N O R T H

S E A

Golspie

Dornoch

Dornoch
Firth

Tarbat
Peninsula

Milton

Dalmore

Cromarty
Firth

Garve

M o r a y
F i r t h

Black
Isle

Dingwall

Loch
Luichart

Inverness

Inverness and
the Black Isle
pages 16–45

Loch Ness

N

0 kilometres   10

0 miles   10

Practical Information

For those after a seamless road trip, read on – this section covers the practicalities of tackling the North Coast 500.

When to go

While most people take to the route during the summer months, there's no right or wrong time to go, with each season offering something different. Ultimately, it all depends on the type of trip you want.

Summer
Summer in Scotland offers the promise of warmer weather and never-ending days, especially in the far north. This inevitably means more people on the route, however, with July and early August especially busy. It pays to book ahead for vehicle hire and accommodation, and for more popular sights and places to eat.

Scotland's infamous midges – tiny biting insects – also love summer. Find out how to tackle them on *p13*.

Spring and autumn
The two shoulder seasons see fewer folk travelling, meaning both the route and the sights along it are quieter. The weather is still relatively good, but rain, wind and mist are more likely. Some sights and businesses might be closed or have shorter opening hours, so detailed planning is essential.

Winter
Surprisingly, winter can be a good time to do the route. For one thing, there'll be hardly another soul travelling, with roads much quieter, and some great deals to be had on accommodation. For another, the winter skies are perfect for stargazing and spotting the northern lights, especially along the less inhabited north coast.

Yet there are downsides. Some sights close between October and April or have reduced hours; accommodation and places to eat can be thin on the ground; and the days are cold and short, with a higher risk of ice, snow and storms. Planning is key, whether it's checking sights are open or bringing lots of warm clothes.

Timings

While a week is long enough to get around the route, two or three weeks is better, allowing you to really immerse yourself in the communities, history and landscapes along the way. And remember: there's no need to complete the route in one go. Instead, why not use it as a jumping-off point for exploring the Highlands?

Getting there

There are several ways to get to Inverness, the route's starting point. Bringing your own vehicle? Jump to the "Arriving by car" section. Hiring one or cycling? Read on.

Arriving by air
Daily flights run from many London airports to Inverness, as well as from Bristol

in southwest England and Cardiff in Wales. Flights from across the UK go to Glasgow, Edinburgh and Aberdeen, from where you can take the train north. Note that while flights within the UK tend to be relatively cheap – especially if you book in advance – airlines charge for hold luggage and additional gear like bikes.

For international travellers, most flights to Inverness require a connection in London or Amsterdam. See the **UK Government** website for details on passports and visas.

UK Government
W gov.uk

Arriving by train

Excellent rail connections run between Inverness and other cities in the UK, with direct trains from London, Aberdeen and Edinburgh. See **National Rail** for information on tickets and timetables, including for ScotRail, Scotland's main train operator.

Travelling from London? The overnight **Caledonian Sleeper** is an option. Rooms are pricey, but you'll save on accommodation. For those on a budget, book a seat-only ticket (cheaper but less comfortable).

National Rail
W nationalrail.co.uk

Caledonian Sleeper
W sleeper.scot

Arriving by coach

Coach services run by the likes of **FlixBus** are a cost-effective option. Regular services run to Inverness from Edinburgh, Glasgow and Aberdeen, costing as little as £10 if you book in advance.

Travelling by coach from London is also possible, with advance tickets coming as cheap as £40. But what you'll save in money, you'll pay for in time – the journey takes around 15 hours and may require a change in Edinburgh, Glasgow or Perth.

For those cycling, Flixbus is often able to transport your bicycle on a carrier on the back of the bus or in the luggage section beneath a special cover (book ahead).

FlixBus
W flixbus.co.uk

Arriving by car

Driving journey times to Inverness can range from manageable (Inverness is only 3 hours from Edinburgh) to wearily long (it's 11 hours from London). Wherever you're starting, plan regular stops along the way to help with fatigue, remembering that there will be fewer services the further north you go. Also note that while parts of the A9 – which runs from north of Stirling to Thurso via Inverness – is dual carriageway, other parts are single carriageway and can become very busy.

Transport on the road

When it comes to your mode of transport, there are a few options to consider, each with their own pros and cons.

Car

It's much easier to navigate the route's roads *(p11)* in a smaller vehicle, but if you're planning to hire a car, prices can be expensive (rising up to £900 a week in summer). And, unlike with a campervan, you'll need » to fork out for accommodation. The communities en route will thank you for the latter, though, with every night's stay putting pounds back into the local economy.

Big hire companies operate at Inverness airport. You'll need to be at least 21 years old (for some hire firms it's 25) and have held a valid licence for at least a year. Make sure the insurance covers 24-hour emergency call-outs – garages are uncommon on some sections. If you're planning to go off road, ensure your car is a 4WD.

Motorbikes

Travelling via motorbike is a popular option, with the route's winding roads providing an exhilarating challenge. **NC500 Moto Experience** offers bike hire; you'll need to be at least 24 years old to hire a 600cc or above and have held your licence for two years. As with cars, make sure your insurance covers call-outs.

NC500 Moto Experience
W nc500motoexperience.co.uk

Campervans, caravans and motorhomes

A campervan (in any form) is a popular choice on the route. It's cheaper, too, with the bulk of your transport and accommodation costs rolled into one. But negotiating the route's roads is trickier, especially if you're in a larger vehicle. In fact, some sections are off-limits to motorhomes more than 5 m (16 ft) in length, including the Bealach na Bà and B869 Drumbeg Road; take the signposted detours. Ignoring this can cause you stress and lead to issues for locals; if a road is blocked, it might prevent folk getting to work or stop emergency services providing help to those in need.

Waste Not, Want Not

If in a campervan or motorhome, it's important to know how to dispose of your waste. Emptying grey water or chemical loo waste at public toilets is a hard no, as it upsets local sewage systems. Luckily, CaMPA has a list of official cassette emptying points on its website (*campa.org.uk/waste-disposal*). Most campsites offer these facilities, too.

There are a couple of other things to bear in mind. Those choosing van life will need to be confident drivers, especially when it comes to reversing (an important skill on the single-track roads, where you might need to reverse into a passing place). And while accommodation costs are lower, it's still best to stay in designated campsites; hunkering down for the night in a passing place is a big no-no, as is taking up valuable space in local car parks.

Local hire companies include **Inverness Campervans** and **North500 Motorhomes**.

Inverness Campervans
W inverness-campervans.co.uk

North500 Motorhomes
W north500.co.uk

Cycling

Many cyclists tackle the route in ten days, averaging roughly 80 km (50 miles) a day, although it depends upon individual preference and ability. Heading clockwise is a good shout (opposite to the chapters in this book), as it avoids the headwinds that plague the west coast.

Advance planning is key. Before setting off, ensure your bike is in good condition and is capable of carrying your kit. Good gearing is a must – there are steep climbs – as is basic bike-repair knowledge and kit, since bike shops are few and far between. OrangeFox offers a mobile repair service.

OrangeFox
W orangefoxbikes.co.uk

Rules of the road

Scotland has many of the same rules of the road as the rest of the UK. Drive on the left; this applies for passing places on single-track roads, too, which can be on either side of the road. If the passing place is on the right side, then pull over to the left just opposite. Passing places are often marked with a white square- or diamond-shaped signpost. The vehicle closest to the nearest passing place is usually the one to pull in, even if it means reversing a short distance. Never park in passing places (they must be kept clear at all times) or block roads that provide access to farm traffic. When parking, it's best to use designated spaces.

Seat belts must be worn at all times and children must travel with the correct child restraint for their weight and size. Mobile phones must not be used while driving, except with a hands-free system.

Avoid drinking any alcohol if you plan to drive. The legal alcohol limit in Scotland is 50 mg of alcohol per 100 ml of blood (0.05 per cent BAC), so just one glass of wine or beer could set you over the limit.

Visit **Road Safety Scotland** for further information, including speed limits according to vehicle type.

Road Safety Scotland
W roadsafety.scot

Road conditions

Roads on the route are a mixed bag. Some, especially on the east coast, are straight and wide; others, including those to the north and west, can be winding and shrink to single-track roads in some parts. Drivers need to be vigilant, especially if contending with sharp bends and blind summits. Single-tracks can be potholed, with high drop-offs at the curbside; steer clear of the edges to avoid punctures. Other road hazards to watch out for are animals on the road and fast-changing weather conditions.

If travelling in high season, expect the roads to be busy, with convoys of caravans sometimes causing delays; be patient and only overtake when it's safe to do so. The same is true when passing vulnerable road users, such as walkers, horse riders and cyclists; pass them slowly, providing as much room as you would for a car.

If cycling, ride in a position where drivers can see you. Avoid stoppping on sharp corners and hill crests. Wear fluorescent clothing and use lights at night and in bad weather; always wear a helmet.

Traffic Scotland provides information for all road users on weather conditions, road networks and current incidents. »

Traffic Scotland
W trafficscotland.org

Fuelling up

Larger towns will have petrol stations, but smaller, more rural places might not. Plan ahead using **Petrol Map** and top up when you can. If travelling in an electric vehicle, check charging stations ahead of time via **Charge Places Scotland**.

Petrol Map
🅦 petrolmap.co.uk

Charge Places Scotland
🅦 chargeplacescotland.org

Navigating

Brown signposts mark the route, providing guidance at most major junctions and turn-offs. Most major sights are signposted, too, but smaller sights might not be, so good navigation tools are essential.

In this guide, we've included **what3words** (w3w) addresses for every sight. One of the most precise ways you can navigate, w3w divides the world into 3-m squares, with each square allocated a unique three-word address. Where possible, we've provided exact w3w addresses for sights, although for more off-the-beaten-track spots, such as beaches and waterfalls, we've given the address for the car park. The app can be used offline, with options to navigate from your current GPS location to a specific w3w address – so handy for areas without mobile phone or Wi-Fi signal. Google maps is also an option (you can link to it from w3w); download maps in advance to use offline.

what3words
🅦 what3words.com

Mobile phones and Wi-Fi

Most of the UK's main providers cover the Highlands, but that doesn't mean you'll always have signal, especially in rural areas.

Wi-Fi hotspots aren't really a thing on the route, but cafes and restaurants usually offer their Wi-Fi password if you make a purchase. Visitors travelling to the UK with EU tariffs can often use their devices without being affected by roaming charges, but check with your provider in advance.

Food, drink and supplies

There are plenty of restaurants and cafes along the way, although there's less choice in more rural areas. Inverness, Tain, Wick and Ullapool have supermarkets. Larger shops are few and far between elsewhere, but it's not an issue, given the availability of local shops, delis and farm stores – plus, buying from these places helps put funds back into the local community.

Many cafes, shops and restaurants have longer hours in summer, but close or have reduced hours from October to April; some close on Sundays and public holidays, too. Big supermarkets tend to stay open later.

Accommodation

Scotland has accommodation to suit all budgets and tastes. The Visit Scotland and North Coast 500 websites *(p15)* both list lots of options. We've also included some extra-special places in this book.

It's best to book ahead, especially in high season. Some places close between

October and April, so always check ahead. Wild camping on most unenclosed land (ie not farmland) is allowed in Scotland, but only for those using non-motorized forms of transport, such as walking or cycling; parking your campervan by the edge of the road is not allowed. The Scottish Outdoor Access Code *(p15)* has more information.

Walkers can also use bothies – basic croft-style houses. They're often free, but are without water, electricity or bedding, so bring supplies. See the **Mountain Bothies Association** for guidance.

Mountain Bothies Association
W mountainbothies.org.uk

Health

Scotland's healthcare system is world-class, with Inverness home to well-equipped Raigmore Hospital. Several smaller hospitals can be found on the east coast, with Thurso's Dunbar Hospital on the north coast. Elsewhere, the main medical centres are doctor's surgeries and pharmacies. **NHS Inform**, the National Health Service website, has a list of medical centres. For minor ailments go to a pharmacy (often open 9am–5pm). Alternatively, call NHS 24 on 111.

Emergency treatment is usually free for UK residents, and there are reciprocal arrangements with Australia, New Zealand and some others (check NHS Inform for details). EU citizens are also eligible for free emergency care provided they have a valid European Health Insurance Card (EHIC). For all other travellers, we recommend taking out a comprehensive insurance policy that includes medical care.

Tap water is safe to drink, unless otherwise stated. If sourcing water from a river or similar, use some sort of filtration system.

Various insects can pose health issues, including midges, tiny insects whose bites may cause itching. They're often active from mid-May to September, appearing at dawn, dusk and during still weather. The best defence is wearing long-sleeved shirts and trousers, and a midge hood (a netted hood that goes over your face and neck). Other insects to watch out for are ticks, which are found in heather, bracken and long grass. These little blood-suckers attach to your skin (or your dog's), often without any sign. They can carry diseases such as Lyme disease, so check yourself regularly and extract promptly with a tick-removing tool if you find one.

It's crucial to bring the right kit with you, including a well-stocked first-aid kit. And take warm clothes, even in summer – the weather can turn in the blink of an eye.

NHS Inform
W nhsinform.scot/scotlands-service-directory

Personal security

While the Highlands are generally safe, it pays to take the usual precautions, such as keeping valuables close. If you have anything stolen, report the crime as soon as possible at the nearest police station; get a copy of the crime report to claim on your insurance. International visitors should contact their embassy or consulate if their passport is stolen or in the event of a serious crime or accident. For emergency services or mountain rescue, dial 999 (or 112). »

Scots are generally accepting of all people, regardless of their race, gender or sexuality. LGBTQ+ rights are mainly in line with the rest of the UK, which are considered among the most progressive in Europe. Same-sex marriage was legalized in 2014 and Scotland is the world's first country to include LGBTQ+ history and education in the school curriculum. The Highlands doesn't have much of an LGBTQ+ scene, but locals are generally positive towards the community. If you ever need support, call the **LGBT Health and Wellbeing** helpline or visit its website.

LGBT Health and Wellbeing
☎ 0300 123 2523
Ⓦ lgbthealth.org.uk

Travellers with specific requirements

Parts of the route can be a challenge for travellers with reduced mobility, with some historic sights and outdoor attractions not accessible. Fortunately, there are places making efforts to open the experience to all. Adapted rooms are available at some hotels, inns and B&Bs – check individual websites – and car-hire firms at Inverness airport offer cars with hand controls at no additional charge; **Enterprise** has vehicles with space for wheelchairs. In terms of the outdoors, **Able 2 Adventure** offers accessible activities, such as canoeing and walking. **Forestry and Land Scotland** has information on all-ability walks and easy-access facilities, while Dornoch beach hires out wheelchairs designed for use on sand *(p56)*.

For further information, **Euan's Guide** has reviews written by travellers with specific requirements on things like toilets, cafes and accommodation. **Capability Scotland**, the country's largest support organization for disabled people, is also a useful resource.

Enterprise
Ⓦ enterprise.co.uk

Able 2 Adventure
Ⓦ able2adventure.co.uk

Forestry and Land Scotland
Ⓦ forestryandland.gov.scot

Euan's Guide
Ⓦ euansguide.com

Capability Scotland
Ⓦ capability-scotland.org.uk

Money

Britain's currency is pound sterling ($£$). Scottish notes look different to English ones, but all are legal tender. Major credit, debit and prepaid currency cards are accepted at most major sights, and in many restaurants and cafes, as are contactless payments. Do carry some cash, though, especially in rural areas – the journey to Cape Wrath, for instance, is cash-only.

Language

English is the official language in Scotland. Gaelic is also spoken, although mainly in the Western Isles. Many spots along the route may have Gaelic names, especially on the west coast, and you'll see road and station signs in Gaelic all over Scotland.

Visitor information

There are plenty of resources available for road trippers, including the official **North Coast 500** website, which features an interactive map.

Other resources include **Visit Scotland**, the country's official tourist website, which has information on the Highlands, plus a searchable accommodation guide. There's also the still-expanding **Be Local** website, run by Scottish Community Tourism; it provides tips on how to be a "temporary local" and includes a searchable map of community-focused spots. Several towns and villages on the route have on-the-ground information centres, such as Gairloch's excellent GALE Centre *(p166)*.

North Coast 500
W northcoast500.com

Visit Scotland
W visitscotland.com

Be Local
W belocal.scot

Scotland's great outdoors

In Scotland, everyone has the right to access the country's open land and waters, providing that they act in a responsible way. The **Scottish Outdoor Access Code** (SOAC) provides in-depth information on

how to do the latter, especially on leaving no trace. The code also applies to historical sights, such as Clava Cairns *(p24)*.

The area's **Countryside Rangers** are an invaluable source of information on the area's outdoors, offering guided walks and other activities, including volunteering. **WalkHighlands**, meanwhile, is an incomparable resource for hikers, providing detailed information on walking routes.

Scottish Outdoor Access Code
W outdooraccess-scotland.scot

Countryside Rangers
W highlifehighland.com/rangers

WalkHighlands
W walkhighlands.co.uk

Leave No Trace

Litter: Always take rubbish home with you or dispose of it in "Keep Scotland Beautiful" bins on the route.

Fires: Avoid open fires, including BBQs, during the drier months or next to forests, farms or peaty ground. When cooking food, it's best to use a camping stove.

Wildlife: Keep your distance from wildlife. If travelling with a dog, ensure they're on a lead, especially around farm animals and during bird breeding seasons.

Toilets: The Highland Council website *(highland.gov.uk/tourism)* has a list of public toilets. If there are no facilities nearby, visit the SOAC website for advice.

INVERNESS AND THE BLACK ISLE

Start Inverness

≫

End Dingwall

Left One of the standing stones
at the edge of Clava Cairns

INVERNESS AND THE BLACK ISLE

The North Coast 500 starts in Inverness, the biggest city in the Highlands. While it might be tempting to hit the road straight away, it pays to spend a couple of days exploring the Highland capital and its nearby sights, among them Culloden Battlefield and Loch Ness. When it's finally time to set off, the road loops west around the edge of the Moray – pronounced "Murray" – Firth, before skirting the Black Isle just north of Inverness. Despite its name, this patchwork of fertile fields is a peninsula, home to pretty seaside villages, gushing waterfalls and some of the country's best dolphin-watching opportunities, so take some time to linger.

Loch Luichart
Loch Garve
Meig
Conon
Orrin
Orrin Reservoir
Beauly
Cannich
Glen Affric
Invermoriston
Dundreggan Rewilding Centre
Fort Augustus

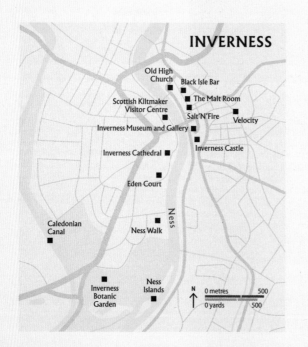

INVERNESS

Old High Church
Black Isle Bar
The Malt Room
Scottish Kiltmaker Visitor Centre
Salt'N'Fire
Velocity
Inverness Museum and Gallery
Inverness Castle
Inverness Cathedral
Eden Court
Ness
Caledonian Canal
Ness Walk
Inverness Botanic Garden
Ness Islands

N
0 metres 500
0 yards 500

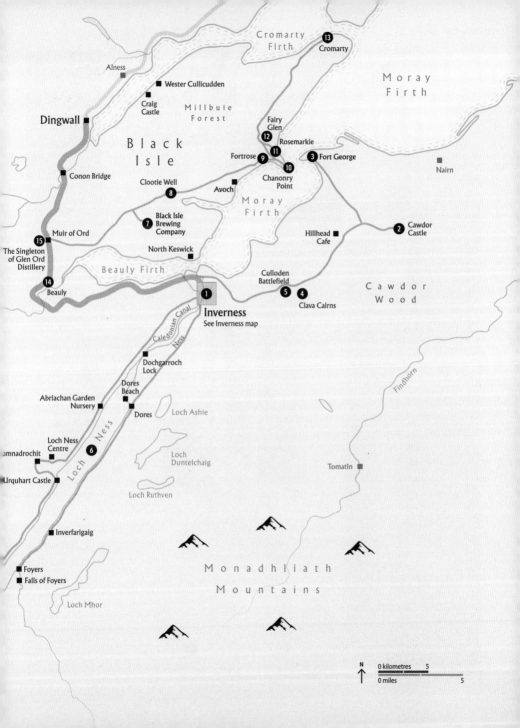

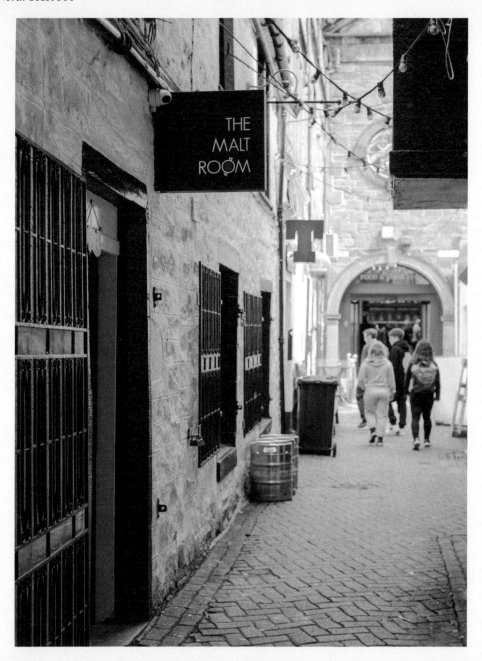

● Inverness

It might be the Highland capital, but historic Inverness feels more like a town than a city. This compact spot has been inhabited for at least 8,500 years, transforming from an important maritime port during the medieval period to a hub of the Highland cattle trade in the 18th century. In the Victorian era, it emerged as a burgeoning tourist destination – something that remains true today, especially as Inverness marks the start and end point of the North Coast 500. This unassuming city is a great place to prepare for the trip ahead, with lots of supermarkets and outdoor shops dotted around. But it's also got plenty to say for itself, with an array of buzzing cafes, restaurants and bars to check out.

The city also has more than its fair share of great sights, which straddle both sides of the broad river from which it takes its name ("Inbhir Nis" in Gaelic means the mouth of the River Ness). One of the best is the **Inverness Museum and Gallery**, tucked up curving Castle Wynd. Spiralling upwards from the ground floor, the museum's exhibits touch on everything from geology and archaeology to social and cultural history, with items on display including carved Pictish stones, taxidermied animals and Jacobite memorabilia. The art gallery, meanwhile, features temporary exhibitions from local creators and internationally renowned artists, such as the Scottish Colourists.

A short stroll uphill from here is pinkish-hued **Inverness Castle**. Built in 1836 on the site of a 12th-century castle, this red-sandstone stronghold is currently closed for a major renovation. On its reopening (expected in 2025), an interactive experience will delve into the landscape, heritage and culture of the Highlands, as well as look to the area's future as a potential leader in areas such as community land development and green energy. Topping it off will be a new viewpoint on its battlements, looking over the city and surrounding scenery. »

Inverness Museum and Gallery
///drips.author.memory 🄰 Castle Wynd
🄲 Hours vary, check website 🅆 highlifehighland.com

Inverness Castle
///sticky.script.maple 🄰 View Place 🄽 For renovation
🅆 invernesscastle.scot 🄵 🄲

Fancy a wee dram? Head to
The Malt Room (////metro.bonus.works; themaltroom.co.uk). Tucked away down a tiny alley off busy Church Street, this cave-like bar is all about the "water of life", with over 350 different whiskies on offer. There's a focus on Scottish malts, naturally, but you can also sample spirits from Japan, Ireland and the USA.

Left The cosy Malt Room, found down a side alley off Church Street and serving up an excellent selection of whisky

North of the castle lies the **Old High Church**. It was built in 1171 on the site where, in the 6th century, St Columba – an Irish missionary who helped spread Christianity in Scotland – converted the Pictish King Brude. The church's most dramatic event took place in the 18th century when Jacobites, following defeat at the battle of Culloden *(p28)*, were first imprisoned inside the building and then later executed by firing squad in its walled graveyard – the walls and graves still bear traces of gunshot holes. Sadly, the church was sold in 2023 and today its future remains uncertain.

South of the castle are the **Ness Islands**, a collection of natural islets in the middle of the river cloaked by mature beech, sycamore and Scots pine trees. Several Victorian footbridges link the islands to each other and to both the east and west riverbanks, making it an accessible and lovely place for a stroll. Keep a close eye on the river while walking; you might see seals, seabirds and – if you're lucky – otters.

Over on the river's west bank is the informative, if touristy, **Scottish Kiltmaker Visitor Centre**, where skilled kiltmakers put on demonstrations, and the double-towered **Inverness Cathedral**, known for its vaulted wooden ceiling, exquisite carvings and stunning stained-glass windows. Just around the corner »

Old High Church
///vines.hips.detail 🏠 Church Street
🕐 Church: closed; graveyard: 24 hrs daily

Ness Islands
///edit.dive.stop 🏠 Great Glen Way 🕐 24 hrs daily

Scottish Kiltmaker Visitor Centre
///patch.offers.punt 🏠 4–9 Huntly Street 🕐 9am–10pm daily 🌐 highlandhouseoffraser.com ♿ 🎫

Inverness Cathedral
///tube.rests.quiz 🏠 Ardross Street 🕐 9am–6pm daily 🌐 invernesscathedral.org ♿ Donation 🎫

The buzzing **Black Isle Bar** (////looked.camera.parade; blackislebrewery.com) serves up some of the best pizzas in Inverness, as well as a vast selection of organic beers made by the Black Isle Brewing Co *(p36)*. If there's no room to sit downstairs, head to the rooftop garden area, which has heaters to fend off the cold – the beers help with that, too.

At the top of cobbled Stephens Brae, bright and airy **Velocity** (////dined.known.giant; velocitylove.co.uk) makes a great pitstop. Expect ethically sourced coffee and local, seasonal grub, including sweet treats. The best thing, though, is the social focus, with an on-site bicycle workshop and events like group bicycle rides.

Inside the city's Victorian Market – an old-school spot filled with shops – is a hall lined with food counters. The pick of the bunch is the vegan **Salt 'N' Fire** (////talent.actors.rating; saltandfireinverness.hungrrr.co.uk), whose delicious grab-and-go meals include veggie-packed wraps and moreish wontons.

Clockwise from top left Pouring a pint in the Black Isle Bar; the sign outside the bar; enjoying a tea and a rocky road inside Velocity; the exterior of the cafe

Looking for a dose of Highland hospitality? Riverside **Ness Walk** (///vision.deny.ballots; nesswalk.com) has it in spades. As well as comfortable rooms and a sophisticated bar, this intimate five-star hotel is home to the fine-dining Torrish Restaurant, which uses local produce in its dishes – including ingredients grown in the hotel's grounds.

from the cathedral is **Eden Court**, a performing arts space containing a theatre and cinema. During summer it hosts the Under Canvas festival, where a variety of acts, including local musicians, perform on the lawns outside Eden Court.

Further south along the river's western bank is **Inverness Botanic Garden**, a diminutive spot that bursts with colour. Alongside a topical hothouse and a cactus garden, it's the site of the G.R.O.W. Project. Over the past 20 years this garden has been transformed by keen gardeners – many of them adults with special needs – from an unloved patch of wasteland to a vibrant oasis, home to vegetable beds, bug hotels and wildflower meadows. From here, it's not far to the **Caledonian Canal**, which runs parallel to the River Ness all the way to lochs Dochfour and Ness. Created in the 19th century by Thomas Telford, the celebrated Scottish civil engineer, this feat of human ingenuity stretches along the length of the Great Glen *(p30)* and connects lochs Ness, Oich, Lochy and Linnhe. It was hardly used for its original purpose as a trade route, since the advent of railways made it redundant, and today is plied

by all sorts of pleasure boats, including **Jacobite Loch Ness Cruises**. For those wanting a gentle walk or a jog, the shady towpath alongside the canal is the answer, with the chance to glimpse local wildlife like herons and kingfishers a bonus.

Eden Court
///mimic.intrigued.slim Bishops Road, Inverness Hours vary, check website eden-court.co.uk For theatre performances and cinema showings

Inverness Botanic Garden
///exam.sage.sharp Bught Lane, Inverness 9.30am–3.45pm daily highlifehighland.com

Jacobite Loch Ness Cruises
///warriors.dragon.videos Dochgarroch Lock On-site Hours vary, check website jacobite.co.uk   Included in cruise

❷ Cawdor Castle

///routs.fools.plums 22.5 km (14 miles) northeast of Inverness On-site Late Apr–early Oct: 10am–5pm daily cawdorcastle.com

From Inverness, a winding single-carriageway road leads to Cawdor Castle. Built in the 14th century for the Thane (clan chief) of Cawdor, this turreted building – more manor house than castle proper – sits amid lush woodland. The interior is rather lavish, with an imposing stone fireplace in the dining room, rare Flemish tapestries in one of the bedrooms and regal portraits in the drawing room. Even the kitchen draws the eye, thanks to its vaulted ceiling and collection of antique cooking items.

Yet it's the colourful gardens and vast forest that are the real stars of the show. There are three gardens in total: a walled garden, once the original kitchen garden for the castle, but today home to beautiful flowerbeds and a collection of sculptures; a 19th-century flower garden, filled with everything from lavender to lilies; and the wild garden, full of rare species from the Himalayan region planted by the 5th earl of Cawdor. It's a great place to be during summer, when open-air theatre shows are staged in the gardens.

Surrounding the castle is Cawdor Big Wood, an ancient parkland cut through by two interlinking burns and filled with oak, pine and lime trees, as well as rare wildlife such as red squirrels. Over 17 km (10 miles) of walking trails make it a joy to explore, including paths through less visited woodland. If you ever need to find your bearings, follow the nearest burn downstream to make your way back to the castle.

Found between Inverness and Cawdor Castle in the new-build town of Tornagrain, **Hillhead Cafe** (///obligated.handy.pirates; 3 School Road, Tornagrain) is the place to go for a refined brunch, with the decadent French toast a real highlight. It's by no means a one-trick pony, though: this stylish spot is equally great for a treat-yourself morning coffee, complete with tasty housemade pastries, or a creative dinner and a cool cocktail come evening.

❸ Fort George

///mimic.intrigued.slim 🚗 20 km (12.5 miles) from Inverness 🅿 On-site 🕐 Apr–Sep: 9.30am–5.30pm daily (last entry 4.30pm); Oct–Mar: 10am to 4pm daily (last entry 3pm) 🌐 historicenvironment.scot ♿
🎧 Audio guide using own phone

About 16 km (10 miles) east of Inverness, the A96 intersects with the Military Road (aka the B9006). This straight marching route leads to an imposing fort, built by King George II following the Battle of Culloden (p28). Situated on a headland in the Moray Firth, it encloses an area the size of five football pitches and was constructed in a star shape, so the soldiers could keep watch on all sides. The fort was never used for its main purpose, as a base to challenge Jacobite uprisings, because by the time it was completed – 23 years after the Battle of Culloden – the threat this group posed was no more. Still, it's housed British army forces for the 250 years since and remains an army barracks today.

Inside, there's a path around the main rampart (stretching 1 km/0.6 miles), from which walkers might glimpse dolphins, minke whales and orcas gliding through the firth. Other highlights include the Highlanders Museum, home to a huge collection of military artifacts recounting the history of Highland troops, and the grand magazine, originally designed to contain over 2,500 gunpowder barrels, but now home to a huge collection of weapons, including pikes, swords and bayoneted muskets. There's even a dog cemetery (one of only two in Scotland), where the likes of officers' dogs and regimental mascots have been laid to rest.

④ Clava Cairns

///misfits.crackling.resort 🏠 11 km (7 miles) east of Inverness; singposted off the B9006 🅿 On-site

Found off a single-track road close to Culloden Battlefield *(p28)*, this Bronze Age burial ground was among the first sites in the UK to be protected by law, way back in 1882. It's made up of a series of cairns (mounds of rock often used as memorials) and standing stones. The site has stood both the test of time – it's around 4,000 years old – and the heavy-handed attention of Victorian antiquarians, who were less than careful while carrying out initial excavations.

There are two sections to Clava. While the smaller Milton of Clava, home to a cairn and a medieval chapel, is impressive, the larger Balnuaran of Clava is the most striking. Here, nestled amid a grove of trees, ancient stone circles sit next to a series of lichen-covered cairns, three of which were built around 2000 BCE. The two larger cairns, located to the northeast and southwest, were constructed with the seasons in mind; on the shortest day of the year, sunlight streams up the passageways of each cairn to illuminate the burial chamber.

There's ancient art at Clava, too: on the southwest cairn, look for circular indents carved into one of the stone slabs. This Bronze Age rock art was first identified in the late 19th century by Christian

McLaggan, one of the first female archaeologists in Britain.

Clava Cairns might be a striking sight, but for a long time it was known only to locals and marauding history buffs. It rose to fame after featuring in the *Outlander* TV show, with avid followers of the series travelling from far and wide to visit (they still do, so it's a good idea to arrive early to secure a parking spot). Some fans previously attempted to take souvenirs from the site home with them, but it's best to leave these ancient cairns in peace.

Above Carved circular rock art marking part of the wall of the southwest cairn

Right One of the larger cairns surrounded by forest

⑤ Culloden Battlefield

///waistcoat.stitching.capillary 🏠 8 km (5 miles) east of Inverness, signposted off the B9006
🅿 On-site 🕐 Moor: daily; Visitor's Centre: Hours vary, check website
Ⓦ nts.org.uk/visit/places/culloden 💷 For museum and tours only; moor free ♿

For many locals, this stretch of moorland, sitting east of Inverness, is the perfect place for a peaceful walk – especially when its posse of singing skylarks swoop through the air and its wildflowers are in full bloom. But such tranquillity belies the moor's violent past: it was here on 16 April 1746 that the infamous Battle of Culloden took place. On this fateful day, King George II's troops, led by his youngest son, the Duke of Cumberland, clashed with Bonnie Prince Charlie's Jacobites, leading to the deaths of around 1,600 men – 1,500 of whom fought for the Jacobite cause. The last pitched battle on British soil, it resulted in Charles Stuart making his famous escape over the sea to the Isle of Skye, with many Highlanders left to suffer bloody reprisals and cultural repression, including the abolition of the clan system.

The moor's first-class visitor centre, which has been designed to blend in with the surrounding landscape, is the place to start. Inside, an interactive, artifact-filled exhibition explains the causes and consequences of the confrontation, and an immersive battle theatre recounts the horror of the day's events. After taking in the exhibition, wander around the moor, where flags mark the position of the two armies, information boards explain the battle in more detail, and a poignant memorial cairn and series of stone markers pay homage to the clans who fought and died. (Some clan graves, especially that of the much-visited Clan Fraser, may be marked off for maintenance; be guided by the staff at the visitor centre.) To get the best out of the visit, a guided tour of the moor, either with one of the museum's expert guides or via the audio tour, is highly recommended.

Clockwise from top Wandering along one of the moorland's wide paths; the memorial marker for the MacGillivray clan; a series of clan memorial markers lining the path

6 Loch Ness

Situated along the Great Glen – a steep-sided valley formed from the twin forces of a geological rift and a glacier – this long body of water is potentially Scotland's most famous loch. It's best known, of course, as the home of the celebrated – and eternally elusive – Loch Ness Monster, fondly called Nessie. But that's not all this loch has going for it: it's also the UK's largest lake by volume, containing within it more water than all of the lakes in Wales and England combined.

A wiggling road runs the full length of the western side of the loch, which is dotted with several interesting spots. There's **Abriachan Garden Nursery**, a tranquil woodland garden that provides an excellent place to stretch your legs, as well as stunning views across Loch Ness. A little further southwest is Drumnadrochit, often called Drum by locals, a pretty village with a shinty obsession – many of the locals play this more hard-core version of hockey. It's home to the **Loch Ness Centre**, which delves into the history of the loch, and the slightly kooky **Nessieland** that, unsurprisingly, is focused on the famous monster. Both places offer tours of the loch and are particularly popular with families. There's also the community-run **Loch Ness Hub**, a welcoming spot that provides visitor information, e-bike hire and more; profits go back into community projects, including a school meal delivery service. »

Abriachan Garden Nursery
///reflector.lists.singer 🏠 14.5 km (9 miles) from Inverness 🅿 On-site 🕒 Feb–Nov: 9am–7pm daily 🆆 lochnessgarden.com

Loch Ness Centre
///scatters.inventors.tens 🏠 Just off the A82 in Drumnadrochit 🅿 On-site 🕒 Hours vary, check website 🆆 lochness.com

Nessieland
///hillsides.nudge.abruptly 🏠 On the A831 in Drumnadrochit, just after the turn-off from the A82 🅿 On-site 🕒 10am–5pm daily 🆆 nessieland.co.uk

Loch Ness Hub
///transmitted.blankets.flop 🏠 Village car park 🅿 On-site 🕒 Hours vary, check website 🆆 lochnesstravel.com

A Drumnadrochit institution, the **Ness Deli** (////joke.grinders.starts; thenessdeli. wordpress.com) is the place to start the day, with everything from porridge and pancakes to full Scottish breakfasts on offer. It also serves up delicious lunches – including hearty Sunday dinners during the winter months – and a whole heap of mouthwatering baking.

Left A tour boat cruising up Loch Ness, its passengers inevitably on the look-out for the fabled Loch Ness Monster

A short drive from Drumnadrochit is **Urquhart Castle**. Despite being in ruins, the castle – once one of Scotland's largest – is still an impressive sight, in part thanks to its lochside location and the soaring remains of its tower house. For some, the castle's ruined state was inevitable; according to local legend, Gaelic nobleman Chonachar Mòr Mac Aoidh forced a coven of witches to build Urquhart in the 12th century; the witches were so enraged that they cursed the castle. Under a spell or not, the castle was passed between multiple groups over the following centuries, including the English and the Scottish MacDonald clan, before being destroyed by government forces during the 17th century. All of this and more is recounted at the visitor centre, where an informative short film covers the castle's long history and medieval artifacts help reimagine how its inhabitants must have once lived. There's also a cafe, plus a rather touristy shop (consider yourself warned) selling the usual "I heart Scotland" mugs and Highland cow tea towels.

Around 27 km (17 miles) south of Urquhart Castle, right at the end of the loch, is Fort Augustus, a quaint hamlet cut through by the Caledonian Canal, an impressive feat of 19th-century engineering – learn all about it at the **Caledonian Canal Heritage Centre**. Fort Augustus also has a host of boat operators offering tours of Loch Ness, as well as self-powered canoe trips from **In Your Element**. »

Urquhart Castle

///replayed.pricing.ratio ⌂ 3 km (2 miles) from Drumnadrochit, just off the A82 🅿 On-site 🕐 Hours vary, check website Ⓦ historicenvironment.scot ♿ ✔ Audio guide using own phone

Caledonian Canal Heritage Centre

///went.unopposed.mice ⌂ Canal Side, Fort Augustus 🕐 Summer: 9am–5pm daily; winter: 9.30am–3.30pm daily Ⓦ scottishcanals.co.uk

In Your Element

⌂ Trip times vary, check website Ⓦ iye.scot

An unusual spot, the **Clansman Centre** (///starting.tomato.testing; clansmancentre.uk) combines a craft-focused giftshop with a re-creation of a traditional Highland turf house. Browse in the shop for Celtic-inspired items, then head to the turf house for a talk; hosted by staff wearing traditional Feilidh Mhor kilts (large, belted pieces of plaid), it covers the clan system, local culture, and Highland dress and weapons.

Clockwise from top Looking towards the ruins of Urquhart Castle; inside Urquhart's gatehouse; view over Loch Ness from the castle

The eastern side of Loch Ness is much quieter than the western side, making it a good spot to escape the crowds. An excellent place to stop off at is **Dores Beach**, a rocky stretch with incredible views south down the loch; it's a great place for a swim, but be warned that the water never feels warm (even the locals swim in wetsuits). About 11 miles (18 km) south are the spectacular **Falls of Foyers**, known in Gaelic as Eas na Smùide (the Smoking Falls). Accessed via a stepped path, this long waterfall tumbles down through pretty woodland roamed by rare red squirrels.

Dores Beach
///worm.swerving.clothed 🅿 On-site, just down from the Dores Inn

Falls of Foyers
///surprise.bookings.outhouse 🅿 Just off the B852, opposite the falls

Found 13 km (8 miles) from Loch Ness's southwestern shore, the Dundreggan Rewilding Centre (///decoder.perfected.smirks; visitdundreggan .co.uk) is the world's first rewilding centre. Run by conservation charity Trees for Life, who are attempting to restore the Caledonian forest that once covered the area, the centre has a fascinating exhibit on rewilding and offers activities such as guided forest walks and tours of the on-site tree nursery. For those wanting to pitch in, sort and sow seeds and pot seedlings during a volunteering week.

Above The picturesque Dores Beach, at the northeastern end of Loch Ness

❼ Black Isle Brewing Co

///among.loitering.hourglass ⌂ Old Allangrange, Munlochy 🅿 On-site 🕙 10am–5pm daily
🆆 blackislebrewery.com 🇮

Back in the late 1990s, avid beer fan and organic-living advocate David Gladwin couldn't find a single organic beer for sale in Scotland. So he decided to make his own, brewing up new creations in a barn on the fertile Black Isle – just across the Moray Firth from Inverness – and selling them to locals from the back of his van.

Fast-forward almost 30 years and Black Isle Brewing Co – known for the catchy motto "Save the planet, drink organic" – has gone on to become an award-winning brand, with its small-batch brews popping up in watering holes across the UK. Brand-name bars have even been established in Inverness *(p20)* and Fort William.

But David hasn't allowed success to go to his head – or change his ideals. The brand is still focused on being fully organic and sustainable, with ingredients that are herbicide- and pesticide-free, and sourced as locally as possible. Even the water used comes from the brewery's own spring, which – as the surrounding farmland is organic – is as unpolluted as you can get.

To top it all off? There's now a market garden out back, which uses regenerative farming techniques to produce organic vegetables, fruit and herbs, which are then sold from a stall here every Thursday or sent to the brewery's bars. The garden even hosts local school children via Flourish, a charity that aims to reconnect children with nature.

Drop by the brewery to learn more on a short-but-sweet 15-minute tour. All aspects of the brewing process are covered, including mashing, fermentation and canning, with the chance to sample a couple of beers in the shop afterwards. Look out for Red Kite – David's first-ever brew and still going strong.

Looking to soak in more of the brewery's wholesome vibe? Spend a couple of nights in its on-site **Shepherd's Hut**. Perched on the edge of the market garden, this handcrafted spot serves up oodles of rustic charm, thanks to its wooden interior and cosy furnishings, complete with tartan blankets. There's a veranda, too, from where you can gaze across fields with a freshly brewed beer in hand.

Clockwise from top left The entrance to the brewery; its market garden, bursting with produce; barrels of beer in the brewery; an array of colourful cans in the on-site shop

● Clootie Well

///conforms.eternally.muddy
North of Munlochy, just off the A832
Hill o Hirdie Wood car park

Found in places with Celtic heritage, such as Ireland and Cornwall, clootie wells have long been associated with healing. According to ancient traditions, if a person dipped a cloot (Scots for a piece of cloth) into a holy well and then tied it to a nearby tree, it would help to cure a sick person, with the illness disappearing as the cloth gradually disintegrated over time.

This particular well – today no more than a small hole in the ground – was first used in early Celtic times, when local people honoured nature spirits with offerings, but later became associated with St Curitan (sometimes known as St Boniface), a Christian bishop during the 7th century.

It's a short walk through woodland to reach the well, which is surrounded by countless pieces of colourful cloth tied to the branches and trunks of neighbouring trees. People still practise this tradition today; if you'd like to leave your own cloot, use a small, biodegradable piece of cloth.

● Fortrose

This seaside town, 16 km (10 miles) northeast of Inverness, is home to a ruined red-sandstone **cathedral**. Once the seat of the bishops of Ross, this striking religious edifice was erected in the 13th century under King David I, but fell into disrepair following the Scottish Reformation. Despite only a small portion of the building remaining, there's still plenty to admire, including the vaulted crypt of the 13th-century chapterhouse and sacristy, plus the post-Reformation clock tower.

Fortrose Cathedral
///fragment.fully.uppermost On the A832 in the burgh of Fortrose Nearby public parking in Fortrose Apr–Sep: 9.30am–5.30pm daily (last entry 5pm); Oct–Mar: 10am–4pm daily (last entry 3.30pm)

● Chanonry Point

///points.runner.airbase Around 2.5 km (1.5 miles) from Fortrose On-site at end of spit

A spit of sand and shingle, Chanonry Point juts out into the Moray Firth between Fortrose and Rosemarkie *(p41)*. Its main draw? It's one of the best places »

Right One of the boat tours that take visitors dolphin-watching off Chanonry Point in the Moray Firth

in the world to see bottlenose dolphins from land.

The often choppy stretch of sea here is squeezed in between the point and the headland where Fort George *(p25)* sits, creating a narrow channel where currents merge. This pushes fish and the dolphins feeding on them closer to the surface, providing the perfect opportunity to glimpse a fin or two.

The firth's bottlenose dolphins are some of the world's largest, at up to 4 m (13 ft) long, and have extra layers of blubber – a necessity in such cold waters – courtesy of the rich feeding grounds here. Numbering around 200, this group is the North Sea's only resident population. For the best chance of seeing them, head to Chanonry Point during a rising tide (the period after low tide, when the tide is coming back in), especially during summer when they come to feed on salmon.

Though you're likely to see dolphins from land, boat tours are available; if you plan to do one, make sure it's approved by the Dolphin Space Programme *(dolphinspace.org)*, which vets operators to ensure they're acting responsibly. Two great options are **Dolphin Spirit**, which sets sail from Inverness *(p20)*, and **Ecoventures**, a tour company based in Cromarty *(p44)*.

Dolphin Spirit
W dolphinspirit.co.uk

Ecoventures
W ecoventures.co.uk

⓫ Rosemarkie

A short drive from Fortrose through fertile farmland is Rosemarkie. This quaint fishing village is best known for its beach, whose peach-coloured sands sweep around the edge of a crescent-shaped bay. The beach is a popular spot with families on sunny days and with walkers year-round – from here you can walk all the way to Chanonry Point *(p38)* or take a side path up to the Fairy Glen *(p42)*. The Countryside Rangers some-times offers seashore safaris along the shore in search of marine wildlife; check out its events page for details *(p15)*.

Along the village's charming high street sits **Groam House Museum**. Set inside in a simple whitewashed building, this small local history museum has a number of intricately carved Pictish standing stones, dating from around the 8th century, whose designs speak about saints and kings. The most famous of them is the Rosemarkie cross-slab, which is covered in enigmatic symbols and crosses. The museum is also home to the nationally recognized George Bain Collection, focused on Celtic-inspired arts and crafts. There's no charge to enter the museum but donations are very welcome.

Groam House Museum
///loft.essay.typhoon 🏠 High Street, Rosemarkie
🅿 Free public parking available a short walk away, where High Street and Mill Road intersect
🕐 1–4pm daily W groamhouse.org.uk

Top left Dolphins jumping out of the water in the Moray Firth
Bottom left Looking towards pretty Rosemarkie from Chanonry Point

⑫ Fairy Glen

///bead.plates.global 🅿 Fairy Glen car park,
signposted off the A832; alternatively, park near
Rosemarkie Beach and walk up

A short drive or a slightly longer walk
leads from Rosemarkie *(p41)* to the Fairy
Glen. Lined by broadleaf trees and moss-
coated rocks, this steep-sided, narrow
valley feels a little otherworldly, especially
in spring when bluebells carpet the forest
floor. Winding through the woodland is a
2-km (1.25-mile) path that follows the
gurgling Rosemarkie Burn to two petite
yet pretty waterfalls, one sitting just
above the other, that cascade down into
peaty pools surrounded by oak, ash and
beech trees. According to local lore, the
glen received its name thanks to children
in the early 20th century, who would
come here to ask the fairies for clean
water. Note that the path up to the falls is
often wet and muddy, so suitable shoes are
a must.

Just before the second waterfall is a
tree trunk studded with coins, previously
placed there by visitors in the hope of
good fortune. Modern-day travellers
should keep their pennies to themselves,
though: the practice can cause pollution,
so simply admire the trunk instead.

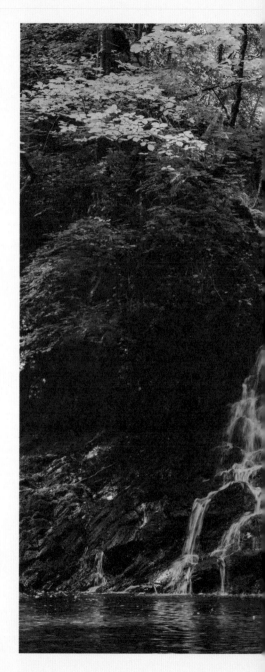

Right The bottom waterfall along
the magical Fairy Glen

⑬ Cromarty

Found at the northwestern tip of the Black Isle, this seaside town is charm personified. Grand Georgian townhouses and humble fishers' cottages stand side by side, while narrow lanes are lined by independent craft shops and art galleries. Somewhat at odds with this pretty picture is a series of small oil rigs rising out of the Cromarty Firth, but even these metal constructions can't detract from the town's beauty.

Cromarty was a prominent port in the 18th and early 19th centuries, fuelled first by the export of salt fish and then by agricultural produce from the fertile soil of the Black Isle, with wealthy merchants contributing to a building boom at the time. However, the town declined during the Victorian period – a devastating blow to those then living there, but something that has allowed it to retain its mid-19th century atmosphere. Today, there are over 200 listed buildings found in Cromarty.

Apart from its striking architecture, the town's main sight is the excellent **Hugh Miller's Birthplace Cottage and Museum**, once home to Cromarty's acclaimed geologist and social reformer. Other places of interest include **Cromarty Courthouse Museum** (a listed building), which recounts the history of the 18th-century courthouse and of the town itself, and the tiny community-run **Cromarty Cinema**, which showcases everything from blockbusters to indie films. There's also ample opportunity to take a walk, from the wooded paths on the South Sutor to the promenade along the beach.

Hugh Miller's Birthplace Cottage and Museum
///logs.placidly.alarmed ⌂ Church Street, Cromarty 🅿 By harbour, then 10-minute walk ⏰ Hours vary, check wesbite 🆆 nts.org.uk 🎟 ⚟

Cromarty Courthouse Museum
///hypnotist.safely.gravitate ⌂ Church Street, Cromarty 🅿 By harbour, then 10-minute walk ⏰ Jul–Aug: noon–4pm daily; Sep–mid-Oct: noon–4pm Wed–Sun 🆆 cromarty-courthouse.org.uk 🎟 Free guided tours at noon and 3pm

Cromarty Cinema
///engraving.illogical.fails ⌂ Next to the ferry slipway, just past harbour 🅿 By harbour, then 10-minute walk 🆆 cromartycinema.com ⚟

⑭ Beauly

Skirting the side of the sparkling Beauly Firth, the North Coast 500 leads from Inverness to this pretty spot. The village is believed to have gained its name in 1564 from the infamous Mary Queen of Scots, who was said to have exclaimed "C'est un beau lieu" ("It's a beautiful place") when she visited. And it is indeed rather picturesque, thanks to its location next to the River Beauly and its collection of old stone houses. The village also holds the slightly strange honour of being home to the shortest railway station platform in Great Britain; it's so small that the door of only one carriage can open to let travellers off.

Claims to fame aside, there's not that much to explore here apart from the **Beauly Priory** – a 13th-century church that remains remarkably grand, despite being in a ruined state – and a handful of excellent shops and cafes. There are plenty of lovely walks in the area, though, especially around the river.

West of Beauly along wooded roads is the sweeping **Glen Affric**. It's widely regarded as one of the most beautiful glens in all of Scotland, thanks to its heather-covered mountains, sparkling lochs and mile upon mile of ancient pine woodlands, a remnant of the vast Caledonian forest that once blanketed much of the country. Walking trails wind through the glen (see WalkHighlands, *p15*); look out for otters, osprey and red deer as you ramble.

Beauly is home to more than its fair share of excellent cafes, but one of the best is **Cafe Biagiotti** (////*elaborate. improvise.anchorman; cafebiagiotti.com*). This Italian coffee shop and *pasticceria* – run by sisters Flora and Rosie, whose mother hails from Tuscany – is the perfect place to break your journey, with everything from antipasti to semifreddo on the menu. Don't miss the focaccia – it's the best in the Highlands.

Another highlight in Beauly is the **Corner on the Square** (////*smokers.schooling.violin; corneronthesquare.co*). A hub for the local community, this family-run cafe-cum-grocer has a big focus on locally sourced produce. Enjoy a meal in the cafe (the generously sized soup-and-sandwich combo is a winner) and then stock up for the rest of your journey in the grocers.

Beauly Priory
///alerting.wages.attention ⌂ The Square, Beauly 🅿 Public parking available on The Square

Glen Affric
///scout.siesta.handlebar ⌂ Around 36 km (22.5 miles) west of Beauly on the A831, then single-track road after Cannich 🅿 Benevean Dam car park

⑮ The Singleton of Glen Ord Distillery

///arose.lazy.financial ⌂ Muir of Ord, Ross-shire 🅿 Large car park on-site; follow the signs from the A832 turn-off 🕐 10am–5pm daily 🌐 malts.com/en-gb/distilleries/ the-singleton-of-glen-ord 🔗 🔗

From Beauly, it's a straight shot along open roads to this famed distillery. Tucked away among the green fields of the Black Isle, the Singleton of Glen Ord has been producing truly delicious whisky ever since it was founded by the local Mackenzie family in 1838.

Covering the distillery's unique "slow craft" process, the tours here feel slick and modern, and range from a straightforward exploration of the distillery – perfect for whisky novices – to a foodie-focused whisky-and-canapé pairing experience. For true aficionados, however, nothing beats the in-depth "Malt to Cask" tour, which explores much more of the distillery complex, including the on-site drum maltings where barley is malted – although for such special access, expect a price point to match.

EAST COAST

Left Sea stacks rising out of the water at Duncansby Head

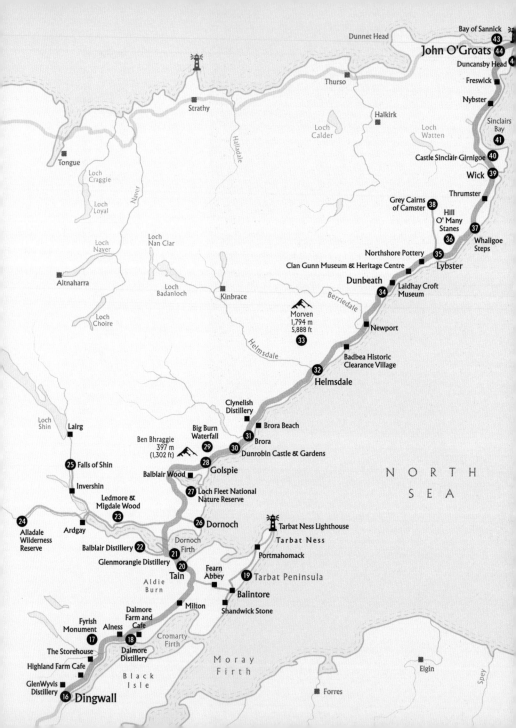

Bay of Sannick **43**
Dunnet Head
John O'Groats **44**
Duncansby Head **4**
Thurso
Freswick
Nybster
Halkirk
Loch Calder
Loch Watten
Sinclairs Bay **41**
Castle Sinclair Girnigoe **40**
Tongue
Wick **39**
Loch Craggie
Thrumster
Loch Loyal
Grey Cairns of Camster **38**
Hill O' Many Stanes **37**
Loch Naver
Loch Nan Clar
Northshore Pottery **35** Whaligoe Steps **36**
Clan Gunn Museum & Heritage Centre
Lybster
Altnaharra
Loch Badanloch
Kinbrace
Dunbeath **34**
Laidhay Croft Museum
Loch Choire
Morven 1,794 m 5,888 ft **33**
Newport
Helmsdale
Badbea Historic Clearance Village
Helmsdale **32**
Clynelish Distillery
Loch Shin
Lairg
Big Burn Waterfall **29**
Ben Bhraggie 397 m (1,302 ft)
Brora Beach **31**
Brora
Falls of Shin **25**
30
Dunrobin Castle & Gardens
Balblair Wood **28**
Golspie
N O R T H
Invershin
Loch Fleet National Nature Reserve **27**
Ledmore & Migdale Wood
S E A
23
Alladale Wilderness Reserve **24**
Ardgay
26 **Dornoch**
Tarbat Ness Lighthouse
Balblair Distillery **22**
Dornoch Firth
Tarbat Ness
Glenmorangie Distillery
Portmahomack
21
20
Fearn Abbey
19 Tarbat Peninsula
Tain
Aldie Burn
Balintore
Milton
Shandwick Stone
Fyrish Monument
Dalmore Farm and Cafe
17 Alness **18**
The Storehouse
Dalmore Distillery
Cromarty Firth
Highland Farm Cafe
B L A C K I s l e
M o r a y F i r t h
Elgin
GlenWyvis Distillery **16** **Dingwall**
Forres
Spey
Strathy
Halladale
Naver
Berriedale
Helmsdale

EAST COAST

After leaving the Black Isle, the route traces the edge of the east coast, first through southeastern Sutherland and then up into Caithness. To begin with, the landscape is pastoral, with farmland bordered by tree- and heather-clad hills to the left and the beach-lined North Sea to the right. But as the North Coast 500 tracks further north, the terrain becomes much flatter and the coastline rises up into cliffs punctuated by "geos", steep-sided inlets where fishers once brought in the catch. This area was once a hub for herring fishing, with villages along the coast dependent on these "silver darlings"; today, heritage centres along the route dive into this history. Take your time over this section: as well as fishing relics, the route is lined with Iron Age brochs (drystone towers), historic castles and a handful of excellent whisky distilleries.

Banff

Fraserburgh

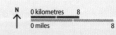

N

0 kilometres   8

0 miles   8

⑯ Dingwall

Despite its diminutive size, this market town is something of a rival to Inverness (especially on the football pitch). In terms of sights, there's little to see, though the **Dingwall Museum** exhibits a modest yet interesting collection of historical finds. Look out for the Mercat Cross, likely constructed to celebrate the town becoming a royal burgh in the 13th century.

Overlooking the town is the Sir Hector Macdonald Memorial. It honours the son of a local crofter who rose through army ranks to become a commanding officer, a role reserved for the upper classes during the Victorian era. On the hill opposite the town is GlenWyvis, a community-owned distillery powered by renewable energy. It doesn't offer any tours, but you can buy its excellent whisky from several shops in the area, including the Highland Farm Cafe.

Dingwall Museum
///regress.beast.valley 🏠 Town House, 65 High Street
🅿 Mayfield car park; 5-minute walk away 🕐 Easter–Oct: 10am–4pm Wed–Sat 🌐 dingwallmuseum.info

Around 5 km (3 miles) from Dingwall, the **Highland Farm Cafe** (///threading.florists. outboard; highlandfarmcafe.co.uk) will fuel you on the journey ahead with its hearty breakfasts and lunches. It's eco-friendly, too, thanks to its solar panels, biomass heating system and EV charging points.

Local, seasonal grub is on offer at **The Storehouse** (////daffodils.grid.herds; thestorehouse.scot), just off the route northeast of Dingwall. Grab a coffee and a cake with views out across the Cromarty Firth, then browse the foodhall and giftshop for local finds to take away.

When the **Dalmore Farm and Cafe** (////gagging.wager.junction; dalmorefarm.co.uk/eat) says local, it means it. Many of the ingredients used in the cafe, a quick stop off the A9, are sourced from local producers, such as scampi from Tain and coffee from roasters in Inverness. And the eggs? From the farm's own chickens, of course.

⑰ Fyrish Monument

///glad.rigs.lorry 🅿 On Boath Road; signposted for B9176, then Boath Road

Around 3 km (2 miles) off the main route is this imposing monument, which sits atop a high, heather-clad hill. It was commissioned by local laird Sir Hector Munro, a commander of British forces in India, following the Highland Clearances *(p102)* as a way of providing an income to those struggling to make ends meet. The monument also celebrates Sir Hector's victory over the Dutch at Negapatam in Madras, with its design thought to have been inspired by the Gates of Negapatam.

Charitable deed or vanity project? We can't be sure. What all can agree on, though, are the spectacular views at the top of the hill, which can be reached via a 6-km (4-mile) walk. The Black Isle's patchwork fields and Cromarty's inky blue firth are laid below, with the hulking form of Ben Wyvis *(p186)* looming to the west.

⑱ Dalmore Distillery

///never.organisms.drape 🏠 Dalmore, Allness
🅿 On-site 🕒 Temporarily for renovations
🆆 thedalmore.com 🔁 🖸

This renowned distillery overlooking the Cromarty Firth has been producing smooth-drinking whisky for over 180 years. Set up in 1839, Dalmore was taken over by descendants of the Mackenzie clan in 1867, who decided to emblazon each bottle with a stag – a nod to their first clan chieftain, Colin of Kintail, who saved King Alexander III of Scotland from being killed by a charging buck.

The distillery is currently undergoing a revamp, with a brand-new visitor experience due to open in 2025. Tours will, of course, be included, giving those visiting a sneak peek into Dalmore's whisky-making process and letting them sample drams of the award-winning amber liquid.

⑲ Tarbat Peninsula

Sitting just off the North Coast 500, this peninsula of fertile fields and sandy shores is definitely worth visiting. Start with the sandy arc of **Shandwick Beach**, found around 25 km (15 miles) northwest of the Dalmore Distillery and a great spot for rockpooling. Nearby is the beautifully carved Shandwick Stone, a large Pictish cross-slab, housed in a protective glass box to shield it from the elements.

Further up the coast is Balintore, a tiny village whose main claim to fame is the **Mermaid of the North**. This 3-m (10- ft)

statue sits upon the Clach Dubh (Gaelic for "black rock") and recounts the story of a mermaid who was caught by a local fisherman and made to be his wife, only for her to eventually escape back to the sea. The statue is part of the area's **Seaboard Sculpture Trail**, which features several other sculptures in the area, including three giant silver salmon (found next to the car park). »

Shandwick Beach
///opinion.kingdom.vacancies 🏠 Off Shore Street, Shandwick 🅿 On-site parking off Shore Street

Shandwick Stone
///slouched.boards.honey 🏠 0.8 km (0.5 miles) from Shandwick, off New Street 🅿 Small parking bay nearby

Mermaid of the North
///echo.slowness.beginning 🏠 On shoreline, close to where Quarry Road meets East Street, Balintore 🅿 Small parking bay on East Street

Seaboard Sculpture Trail
🆆 easterrosspeninsula.com

Balintore's community-run **Seaboard Centre** (///tastings.indulges. lighter; seaboardcentre.com), just north of the *Mermaid of the North* statue, offers hot drinks and some delicious homemade bakes. This spot also runs events such as film nights and live music performances – all of which visitors are welcome to attend – and has facilities, including showers, which you can use for a small donation.

Northwest past fertile fields is 13th-century **Fearn Abbey**, one of Scotland's oldest pre-Reformation churches still in use. Close by is the **Fearn Free Food Garden**, a community spot that sometimes hosts events for visitors wanting to get their hands dirty.

Perched on the tip of the peninsula is the **Tarbat Ness Lighthouse**. This red-and-white striped lighthouse – constructed by Robert Stevenson, uncle of famed novelist Robert Louis Stevenson – is one of the tallest on mainland Britain at more than 40 m (130 ft). It's on private land, but you can take the rough path to the right of it to reach the end of the peninsula. The area around the lighthouse is a Site of Special Scientific Interest (SSSI): the surrounding waters are home to grey seals, otters, bottlenose dolphins and several species of migrating whale, while plenty of birds nest along the shoreline. For those looking to make a positive impact on the peninsula, check with the Countryside Rangers *(p15)*, who sometimes hosts events to clear gorse.

From the lighthouse, narrow roads wind towards Portmahomack, a fishing village whose origins date back to the 6th century CE when the area was a Pictish heartland. The Old Tarbat Parish Church was built on the site of a Pictish monastery and today houses the **Tarbat Discovery Centre**, celebrating the region's Pictish heritage.

Portmahomack's broad beach, which is hardly ever busy, is a perfect sunset spot (it's the only beach on the east coast facing west). The Countryside Rangers run seashore safaris here, while a viewpoint just north is a good place to see marine life.

Fearn Abbey
///purely.custom.weeds 🏠 Signposted off the B9165
🅿 On-site 🕐 Apr–Sep: 10am–4pm daily

Fearn Free Food Garden
///obeyed.snails.interrupt 🏠 Off Main Road, Fearn
🆆 fearnfreefoodgarden.org

Tarbat Ness Lighthouse
///this.handbags.script 🏠 Follow road north from Portmahomack 🅿 Small car park south of lighthouse

Tarbat Discovery Centre
///dwarves.saving.kilowatt 🏠 Tarbatness Road 🅿 On-site
🕐 Hours vary, check website 🆆 tarbat-discovery.co.uk

⑳ Tain

Quiet and unassuming, Tain is often bypassed by visitors in their haste to go north. But it's worth making a pitstop in this market town, in particular to learn about its history at the volunteer-run **Tain and District Museum**.

Southwest of Tain is **Aldie Burn**, a pretty forested area. Two accessible trails wind through pine trees often roamed by pine marten and capercaillie.

Tain and District Museum
///picnic.budding.worksheet 🏠 Tower Street
🅿 On-street nearby 🕐 Apr–Oct: 10am–4pm Tue–Fri
🆆 tainmuseum.org.uk

Aldie Burn
///brambles.saves.gravest 🏠 Signposted off the A9
🅿 On-site 🆆 forestryandland.gov.scot

Clockwise from top The *Mermaid of the North* statue in Balintore; the striking Tarbat Ness Lighthouse; a fisher at work off the coast of the peninsula

㉑ Glenmorangie Distillery

///slouched.boards.honey ⌂ Glenmorangie Distillery, Tain ⓟ On-site ⓣ Jun–Aug: 10am–5pm daily; Sep–May: 10am–5pm Mon–Fri ⓦ glenmorangie.com ⓕ ⓘ

Located on the shores of the Dornoch Firth just north of Tain *(p53)*, this renowned distillery has been turning the holy trinity of water, yeast and malted barley into a smooth, vanilla-tasting whisky for over 180 years. A variety of excellent tours explain the process, from mashing and fermentation to distilling and maturation. A highlight is a stop-off at the "Highland Cathedral" (the stills house): it's home to 8-m- (26-ft-) high stills – the tallest in Scotland – whose long necks inspired the distillery to adopt the giraffe as its logo. Each tour ends, as you'd expect, with the chance to sample a dram or two of single malt under the expert eye of your tour guide, who explains how best to sniff and sip.

Despite producing one of Scotland's most famous whiskies, Glenmorangie doesn't rest on its laurels. The distillery recently built The Lighthouse, a glass-and-steel building that contrasts strikingly with the surrounding stone buildings. This is where Master Distiller Dr Bill Lumsden dreams up new – and as yet unreleased – types of whisky. Cutting-edge technology, including stills whose height can be altered via a water jacket, allow for forward-thinking experimentation. Naturally, it's all very hush hush (so don't expect to see inside).

The folks at Glenmorangie are also passionate about sustainability and regeneration, whether that's transforming whisky casks into surfboards or working alongside the Marine Conservation Society to reintroduce native European oysters back into the Dornoch Firth. This approach is ingrained in the whisky-producing process, too: the leftover barley from the mashing process is either fed to local cows or put through the on-site digestion plant, which creates methane that's used to power the distillery and clean water that's then released into the firth. Want to learn more? Speak to the distillery's enthusiastic staff.

Clockwise from top left Sampling a couple of drams at the end of the tour; the cask warehouse where the whisky matures; the "Highland Cathedral" where the whisky is distilled

㉒ Balblair Distillery

///lance.battle.sidelined ⌂ Edderton, Tain 🅿 On-site
🕐 Apr–Sep: 10am–5pm Mon–Fri, 11am–4pm Sat;
Oct–Mar: 10am–4.30pm Mon–Fri 🆆 balblair.com 🗘 🗗

Sitting around 8 km (5 miles) west of
Glenmorangie (p54), Balblair might
not win against its neighbour in the
size stakes, but it can when it comes
to longevity. This is the area's oldest
distillery, having been founded in 1790.

Perhaps this long-standing history is
why they're so happy to take things slow
here: the fermentation process for Balblair's
fruity yet full-bodied whisky is longer
than usual (62 hours), as is distillation
(4.5 hours). Such patience and care is
also shown when selecting ingredients,
including the top-quality barley sourced
from Black Isle farms and the water that
flows down the hillside nearby. As with
most distilleries on the route, tours
are offered: learn about the whisky-
making process, taste the wort and the
wash, and sample a dram or two.

㉓ Ledmore & Migdale Wood

///simply.ferried.flickers ⌂ 1 km (0.6 miles) from
Spinningdale, 8 km (5 miles) off the A9
🅿 Torroy car park 🆆 woodlandtrust.org.uk

Located on the northern bank of the
Dornoch Firth, this vast area – one of
the Woodland Trust's largest – covers
three SSSIs. Two of these are forested
areas: Ledmore Oakwood, Sutherland's

largest patch of ancient oakwood, and
Migdale Pinewood, likely planted in the
18th and 19th centuries, and mostly made
up of Scots pine and larch. Rounding off
the trio is the peaty Spinningdale Bog,
dotted with willow, alder and birch trees.

Such a diversity of habitats means a
wealth of wildlife, from birds like ospreys
and buzzards to mammals like deer and
pine martens. Look out, too, for a flash of
rusty scarlet. Back in 2019, the Woodland
Trust partnered with Highland conservation charity Trees for Life (p34) to
reintroduce red squirrels here.

Several walking tracks wind through
the area, including one that heads up to the
top of A' Chraisg, a heather-clad moorland
with stunning views over the surrounding
hills. The ranger service (p15) occasionally
offers guided walks in the area.

Fancy doing a good deed while visiting?
The Woodland Trust runs volunteering
events to help improve the health of the
forest (for example, by cutting back
bracken to allow new saplings to thrive).
Check out its website for information.

Want to immerse yourself in the wilderness
without having to camp? Bunking down at
Alladale Wilderness Reserve might be
the ticket. There's a variety of options on
offer, from a couple of cosy cottages to a
luxury Victorian manor, known as Alladale
Lodge, featuring a sauna and snooker room.
While your wallet might not thank you (it's
pricey) your stomach will, with all accommodation fully catered by an on-site chef.

»

㉔ Alladale Wilderness Reserve

///trailing.eager.variances 🅐 19 km (12 miles) from Ardgay village 🅿 Car parking outside Alladale Lodge 🅦 alladale.com

Back in 2003, Paul Lister – heir to the MFI furniture empire and founder of the European Nature Trust – purchased Alladale Estate, a sweeping stretch of wilderness roughly 42 km (26 miles) west of Tain. His vision was simple yet bold: to rewild it.

Today, Paul and his team have planted nearly a million native trees, including Scots pine, aspen, alder and rowan. This work led to a substantial increase in forest cover and a big uptick in biodiversity, with everything from ptarmigan and golden eagles to red squirrels and hares calling Alladale home. Other projects have included restoring the reserve's peaty bogs – a key habitat for capturing carbon and fighting climate change – and breeding rare wildcats for release into the wild. Despite this, Alladale has attracted its fair share of controversy, especially around its desire to reintroduce apex predators, such as lynx and wolves, into the reserve in enclosed areas – something that is a long way off.

The best way to experience Alladale's rich nature is, of course, to get out into it – and thankfully the area offers plenty of opportunities to do just that. A series of trails fan out across the reserve's beautiful hills and glens, including the Glun Liath ridge walk, from where you can admire both Scotland's west and east coasts. The reserve's lochs and rivers are great for wild swimming and there's also excellent mountain biking, with a particularly striking route running along Glen Alladale.

㉕ Falls of Shin

///decorator.teach.robe 🅐 Achany Glen, off the B864, Lairg 🅿 On-site; EV charging point available 🅦 forestryandland.gov.scot

Found north of Balblair on the River Shin, which wriggles its way through wooded Achany Glen, this roaring waterfall is one of the best spots in Scotland to see Atlantic salmon leaping out of the water between May and October. Making their way from the ocean to their nesting ground at nearby Loch Shin, these hardy fish must tackle the 3.5-m (11-ft) falls – hurling themselves upwards using their powerful tails – in order to have a chance of reproducing.

Even if the salmon don't make an appearance, this is still a pretty spot to visit, with several walks available, including a wooded trail and one that runs along the riverside. There's also a cute cafe close to the car park.

㉖ Dornoch

Seaside Dornoch is home to a charming historic centre, filled with independent shops, restaurants and cafes. Its wide streets are lined by sandstone buildings that seem to glow in the sunshine, something that gives the town a warm and welcoming feel.

At the heart of the town is 13th-century **Dornoch Cathedral**. Its name is somewhat of a misnomer, as it was deprived of its cathedral status following the Scottish Reformation (it's now a parish church). Crafted from golden sandstone, it's a striking building, decorated with gargoyles and beautiful stained-glass windows. Those to the north are dedicated to Scottish-American industrialist and philanthropist Andrew Carnegie, who often spent his summers at nearby Skibo Castle. »

Dornoch Cathedral
///dawn.nooks.proven ⌂ St Gilbert Street
🅿 St Gilbert Street ⏱ During daylight hours;
Sunday service 11am Ⓦ dornoch-cathedral.com

If you need a pick-me-up then **Milk & Honey** (///cheered.blank.fortified; 01862 811235) is the place to go. Across the road from the cathedral in a stone cottage, this warm and welcoming cafe serves all the usual suspects for breakfast and lunch. After something sweet? The cakes are incredible.

Right Views across the beautiful sands of Dornoch Beach

A five-minute walk from the cathedral is the **Historylinks Museum**. This celebrated spot showcases the town's long history, stretching from Neolithic times, through to the Picts and the Vikings, and on to the Clearances and beyond. Highlights of the collections include the 13th-century seal of a Dornoch Chaplain and a scull (fishing bait basket) that was once used by the fishing industry's "herring girls" (the women who would gut, salt and pack the fish). For those looking for a further history fix, the museum runs guided walks of the town at 2pm from June to August.

On the eastern edge of town is **Royal Dornoch**, the town's championship golf course. Regarded as one of the best courses in Scotland, if not the world, it's home to two full 18-hole courses and offers incredible views across the firth.

The golf course also overlooks **Dornoch Beach**, a wide expanse of pale golden sand backed by grassy dunes. Thanks to its calm, shallow waters and Blue Flag status, the beach is especially popular with families, who come to paddle in the shallows and search for critters in the rockpools. It's one of the route's most accessible, too, thanks to **Dornoch Beach Wheelchairs**, which provides the free hire of wheelchairs from a building next to the beach car park (book online in advance). Surrounding the beach is an SSSI home to local flora and fauna, such as bird's-foot trefoil and the bar-tailed godwit.

To the beach's southern end is the Gizzen Briggs sandbank, which according to legend is the remains of a magical bridge once constructed by fairies. A little further north of Dornoch Beach lies Embo, another beautiful stretch of sand.

Historylinks Museum
///quilting.clash.hovered 🏠 The Meadows
🅿 Nearby on The Meadows or Shore Road; Blue Badge parking bay available close to entrance
🕐 Apr–Oct: 10.30am–4pm daily
🆆 historylinks.org.uk 🔗 🅒

Royal Dornoch
///blown.mountain.require 🏠 Golf Road
🅿 On-site 🕐 Hours vary, check website; book a tee time online 🆆 royaldornoch.com 🔗

Dornoch Beach
///actor.locked.amending 🏠 End of Golf Road/Beach Road 🅿 Parking just above beach, as well as at end of Golf Road/Beach Road

Dornoch Beach Wheelchairs
///reputable.diamond.watched
🆆 dornochbeachwheelchairs.co.uk

Perched beside Dornoch Beach car park, the unassuming **Highland Larder** (///simply.ferried.flickers; 07368 362379) serves up hefty helpings of delicious seafood, including lobster rolls, hand-dived scallop salads and cajun cod burgers. It's run by Ewan Chisholm, the son of a Dornoch farmer, who sources his seafood fresh from local fishers.

Clockwise from top Seafood lunches from the Highland Larder; Ewan, the owner of the seafood hut; looking out across Dornoch Beach

Top A curlew standing on seaweed
Bottom A seal resting on a rock in the estuary
Right A sign warning of otters on the road through the reserve

㉗ Loch Fleet
National Nature Reserve

///carver.grades.pods 🅿 Skelbo, the Mound, Balblair Wood, Littleferry
🅆 nature.scot

From Dornoch, the road heads north through a mixture of patchwork fields and woodland, eventually crossing this nature reserve, a large estuary with fast-flowing currents. At each low tide, the bean-shaped sea loch is emptied out, revealing sandbars quickly visited by wading birds and seals. Otters and water vole, meanwhile, can be seen along the reserve's coastline.

Other habitats are found elsewhere in the reserve, with Littleferry a popular spot.

Found on the northern side of the estuary's entrance, it's known for its wildflower- and lichen-dotted dunes covered with bumblebees, and a golden beach, which attracts Arctic terns and oystercatchers.

Another of the reserve's habitats is at Balblair Wood, which shares its name with Balblair Distillery *(p56)* but is actually 25 km (15 miles) further north. This forest of Scots pine, situated northwest of Littleferry, is the stomping ground of pinemartens and rare pinewood plants; the Countryside Rangers *(p15)* sometimes offer guided walks in the wood to look for the latter, including one-flowered wintergreen and twinflower.

For those looking to shorten their route, take the A839 northwest from Loch Fleet National Nature Reserve towards the pretty village of Lairg. From here you can either follow the road alongside Loch Broom, heading towards Scourie and the northwest coast, or go straight to the west coast via Knockan Crag *(p144)*. Lairg, perched on the edge of Loch Shin, also makes a great base for exploring different points of the route, with most key spots no more than 90 minutes away by car.

㉘ Golspie

Though the little village of Golspie has a handful of cute shops and an arching golden-sand beach, its reputation for mountain biking is what brings in the visitors. The Highland Wildcat Trails, a series of mountain-biking routes, snake down the slopes of Ben Bhraggie, a 397-m (1,302-ft) mountain overlooking the village, with trails ranging from those suitable for beginners (green) to the more technical for experts (black). The most difficult route runs down from the summit of Ben Bhraggie, and holds the title of the longest free-ride descent in Britain at 13.6 km (8.5 miles).

If mountain bikes aren't your thing, there's a nice walk up to the top of Ben Bhraggie, which is crowned by the Duke of Sutherland monument. Known to locals as "The Mannie", this 30-m- (100-ft-) high statue was raised in honour of George Leveson-Gower, first duke of Sutherland, in 1834. Today, the statue is considered controversial by many. The duke played a significant role in the notorious Highland Clearances during the 19th century, and saw around 15,000 tenants evicted from his vast estate, many of whom were forcibly removed. Given the history, plus the words engraved on the statue (describing the duke as "a judicious, kind and liberal landlord who identified the improvement of the vast estates with the prosperity of all who cultivated them"), some have defaced and attempted to topple the statue; others, however, believe that the monument should be left as a reminder of the past.

㉙ Big Burn Waterfall

///treble.zoos.tonality 🅿 Just north of Sibell Road in Golspie, off the A9

The 3-km (1.75-mile) walk to this tumbling waterfall – found at the end of a long, sometimes steep-sided gorge – is magical whatever the time of year. In spring green leaves burst forth from the deciduous woodland; in spring the forest floor is carpeted by bluebells, wood sorrel and strong-smelling wild garlic; and in autumn the woodland glows with the changing foliage. It's even beautiful in the depths of winter, especially if snow has fallen, though it pays to be careful on the path, which is steep in places.

The trail crisscrosses the stream running through the gorge several times, passing by mini-waterfalls before finally reaching the main event. The fall cascades down inky black rocks into an equally dark pool that's surrounded by moss- and lichen-covered stones. Guided walks to the waterfall, with a focus on the area's rich variety of lichen and moss, are run by the Countryside Rangers *(p15)*. To round off the walk, take a small detour around a little lochan on the way back to the car park or, for those wanting a bigger challenge, hike up to the summit of Ben Bhraggie.

Right The striking Big Burn Waterfall gushing down through lush forest

③ Dunrobin Castle & Gardens

///available.shortcuts.equivocal 🚗 0.8 km (0.5 miles) north of Golspie, Sutherland
🅿 On-site 🕐 Mar, Apr & Oct: 10.30am–4.30pm daily (last entry 4pm);
May–Sep: 10am–5pm daily (last entry 4.30pm) 🆆 dunrobincastle.co.uk 🔗

Situated on a hill overlooking the sea, Dunrobin looks more like an elegant French chateau than your usual imposing Scottish fortification. Yet this confection of a castle began life in the 1300s as a square keep. It was developed and remodelled over the years by the Sutherland family, who have lived here for centuries, and gained its current appearance in the mid-19th century when Sir Charles Barry (architect of London's Houses of Parliament) gave it a makeover. He added the castle's now-famous conical spires, as well as its lavish gardens, based on those found in France's Palace of Versailles. While few could disagree with the end result, which is undoubtedly beautiful, it pays to remember that the castle and garden were only possible due to wealth generated by the brutal Highland Clearances, which saw many crofters evicted from their homes.

Many visitors begin their exploration of the castle in the gardens, which grant beautiful views of the castle. Paths criss-cross the green space, winding past pretty fountains, a croquet lawn and beds full of beautiful blooms. There's even a falconry lawn, where displays take place twice a day (11.30am and 2.30pm). On the northern edge of the gardens is the castle's museum, an eclectic – and somewhat divisive – collection of objects, including family keepsakes, ethnographic items taken from Africa and elsewhere, and an extensive number of hunting trophies (they're not to everyone's taste).

Inside the castle itself, a small selection of rooms are open to visitors. Highlights include the library, lined with bookshelves bursting with over 10,000 tomes, and the drawing room, filled with regal French furniture and 18th-century tapestries. Friendly staff members are on hand to answer questions or just have a general chat about the castle. Many of them are locals and have worked here for years, often following in the footsteps of another family member; it's something that, despite the castle's grandeur, helps give Dunrobin a down-to-earth, community feel.

Clockwise from top left One of the displays at the falconry lawn; the turreted castle; a regal chandelier inside the castle; the lush gardens filled with plants

③ Brora

Just 8 km (5 miles) north of Dunrobin *(p66)*, Brora was once an important place for coal mining, something seen in the stone workers' cottages that line its street. This industrial past is also recounted in the exhibits at the **Brora Heritage Centre**, a small yet engaging local history museum that also covers crofting, the Clearances and the area's role in salt manufacturing. (Note: the centre is due to move location to the refurbished Old Clyne School some time in 2025.)

Skirting the edge of the village next to its golf course is a strip of gold-pink sand, **Brora Beach**. Despite winning awards, it's one of the most deserted beaches on the coast, making it a good place for a tranquil seaside stroll. In fact, a walk winds all the way to Golspie *(p64)*, passing by wave-splashed caves, Carn Liath (an Iron Age broch) and the magnificent Dunrobin Castle. For water-based activities, look no further than the **Sutherland Adventure Company**, which hires out surfboards and body boards, and offers snorkelling trips.

Not far from the village centre is **Clynelish Distillery**. As well as selling its own malts, the distillery partners with Johnnie Walker on its blended whiskies. Tours of the distillery include tastings in a rather stylish bar, which has glorious sea views.

Brora Heritage Centre
///hoops.enhancement.pacemaker ⌂ Coal Pit Road, Fascally 🅿 On-site 🕑 Easter–Oct: 10.30am–4.30pm daily 🆆 clyneheritage.com 🔗 Donation

Brora Beach
///gasp.fronted.correctly ⌂ Short stroll from Golf Road 🅿 Free at golf course

Sutherland Adventure Company
🆆 sutherlandadventurecompany.com 🔗

Clynelish Distillery
///ignites.washed.overcomes ⌂ Just off Clynelish Road 🅿 On-site; also bike racks and EV charging points 🕑 10am–6pm daily 🆆 malts.com/en-gb/distilleries/clynelish 🔗 🔗

The bright pink facade of **Capaldis of Brora** (////town.earplugs.gala; 01408 622713) certainly stands out from the surrounding stone buildings in Brora's village centre. This cute ice-cream parlour has been serving up creamy gelato since 1932 and often creates seasonal flavours, such as cream egg (Easter) and green apple (autumn). Grab a cone before heading down to the beach.

Top right The sweeping and surprisingly quiet sands of Brora Beach
Bottom right A stand-up paddleboarder skimming across the sea

MUSEUM
GALLERY
ARCHIVE
STORY-TELLING
GARDEN
SHOP
RIVER-CAFE

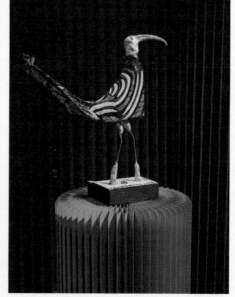

③ Helmsdale

One of the east coast's most picturesque fishing villages, Helmsdale is a quaint collection of stone cottages clustered around a rivermouth harbour. The village was built in 1814 by the duke of Sutherland to house crofting families who'd been removed from inland farms during the Clearances *(p102)*. Today, a modern statue called **The Emigrants**, found in Couper Park, gives a nod to those who decided to leave Scotland in search of a better life. Following the Clearances, many prospered thanks to the herring industry; the village was once home to one of the country's largest fleets fishing for these "silver darlings".

Helmsdale's history is brought to life at **Timespan**, an award-winning heritage centre that's appropriately housed in an old herring curing yard. Set up in the 1980s by three local women, the museum has audio-visual exhibits that touch on the Clearances, the herring industry and the 1869 gold rush that saw prospectors flock to the village's river. Elsewhere, life-sized tableaux provide a window into what life was once like in the village; these were made by members of the community, and in fact many of the items in the collection were donated by locals. There's an art gallery here, too, with exhibitions often focusing on contemporary issues or social movements, as well as a small library, pretty garden, and the all-important gift-shop and cafe; the latter offers excellent crepes and riverside seating.

For more on the Clearances, head 10 km (6 miles) north to **Badbea Historic Clearance Village**. The ruins of this now-deserted cliffside village – whipped by the waves and the weather – are a poignant reminder of those forced to live in difficult conditions following the event.

The Emigrants
///mammoths.rollover.armful ☖ Couper Park
🅿 Layby parking next to the A9, then path

Timespan
///flocking.motivate.discloses ☖ Dunrobin Street
🅿 On-site 🕒 Mar–Oct: 10am–5pm daily
🆆 timespan.org.uk ♿

Badbea Historic Clearance Village
///seatbelt.animator.really ☖ 10 km (6 miles) north of Helmsdale 🅿 Car park next to the A9, then walk in

③ Morven

///giant.managed.amazed 🅿 Small car park near phone box at the end of road to Braemore
🆆 walkhighlands.co.uk

Rising from the relatively flat Caithness landscape, this conical hill provides a rather striking silhouette. The highest peak in the area, Morven is popular with walkers for the incredible views it offers from its summit – on a good day you might see as far as Ben Hope *(p108)* in the north. While it's not particularly high, reaching the top is a tough day-walk, thanks to the hill's steep slopes.

Clockwise from top The tranquil garden at Timespan; one of the artworks on display at the gallery; the entrance to the heritage centre

34 Dunbeath

Just like Helmsdale, Dunbeath was set up following the Clearances and saw a modest boom in the early 19th century thanks to the herring industry. **Dunbeath Heritage Centre** is the main point of interest in the village, providing a thoughtful look at the area's history, as well as information on the life and work of novelist Neil Gunn, who was born here. The *Kenn and the Salmon* sculpture, found close to the harbour, also honours his work.

Around 2.5 km (1.5 miles) north is the **Laidhay Croft Museum**, a traditional thatched longhouse that's now a museum showcasing what life was once like for crofting families during the 18th and 19th centuries. A little further on is the **Clan Gunn Museum & Heritage Centre**. Housed in an 18th-century church, it describes of one of Scotland's oldest Highland clans, taking visitors from Norse times, through the 1745 Jacobite Uprising and the Clearances, all the way to the present day.

Dunbeath Heritage Centre
///longer.bench.defrost 🏠 The Old School
🅿 On-site 🕐 10am–4pm Tue, Wed & Fri
🆆 dunbeath-heritage.org.uk 🔗

Laidhay Croft Museum
///spout.exacts.situation 🚗 2 km (1 mile) north of Dunbeath, just off the A9 🅿 On-site
🕐 Apr–Oct: 10am–4pm daily 🆆 laidhay.co.uk 🔗

Clan Gunn Museum & Heritage Centre
///advances.supreme.amplified 🏠 Latheron, shortly after turning from the A9 onto the A99 🅿 On-site 🕐 Jun–Sep: 11am–4pm Mon–Sat 🆆 clangunnsociety.org/hc 🔗

35 Lybster

Today not much more than a long main street lined by houses, the village of Lybster was once the third-largest herring port in Scotland. Every day, over 350 boats would return to its harbour laden with herring – at the peak of the industry, 50,0000 barrels of this salted fish would be exported from the village each year.

Located next to the harbour, the **Waterlines Heritage Centre** tells the story of the herring boom, alongside somewhat eclectic exhibits covering both the area's fossils and its local bird-life (there's even a live CCTV feed of nesting birds on the Caithness cliffs). There's an excellent cafe, too.

Outside on the harbour – still a port of call for local fishers – is a reconstructed smokehouse and, a little further along, a small lighthouse.

Waterlines Heritage Centre
///quilt.voters.grins 🏠 Lybster Harbour,
Shore Road 🅿 On-site 🕐 May–Sep: 11am–5pm daily 🔗

Housed in a refurbished oatmeal mill south of Lybster, **Northshore Pottery** (*////articulated.earlobe.situation; north shorepottery.co.uk*) is run by local ceramics artist Jenny Mackenzie Ross, who takes inspiration from the area's geology and ecology. Drop by to see what she's working on and pick up a piece to take home.

Above The Hill O' Many Stanes, perched on a small slope on the Caithness coast

③⑥ Hill O' Many Stanes

///driftwood.weaned.arming 🚗 7 km (4.5 miles) from Lybster, just off the A99; signposted on single-track road 🅿 Very small parking bay on single-track road 🌐 historicenvironment.scot

From a distance this patch of heather-covered hillside doesn't look like much at all. But come closer and around 200 small standing stones, arranged in rows, emerge from the earth, stretching south down a gentle slope. According to archaeologists, the site was constructed around 2000 BCE and used to have 600 stones, although its purpose still remains unclear – theories include it being a gathering point for religious ceremonies, an astronomical observatory or a monument to ancestors. Whatever the reason for its existence, such an arrangement of standing stones is rare, with only a handful of other similar sites found across Europe.

Clockwise from top left Davie, the Whaligoe Steps' unofficial caretaker;
Davie getting ready to ride his backwards bike; the steps snaking down towards the harbour

③⑦ Whaligoe Steps

///essay.valley.loitering 🏠 The Haven, just off the A99; signposted
🅿 Car park above the steps

Named after the whales that once washed up here, Whaligoe (meaning an inlet of whales) is one of the east coast's most striking sights. Zigzagging down the edge of a high sea cliff to a rocky inlet that acts as a natural harbour, this series of steep steps was built by Captain David Brodie in the late 18th century. He wanted the harbour – in use since the 1640s – to be more efficiently set up for herring fishing, which saw a boom during the 19th century. Before the steps were built, locals negotiated a rough track with a sheer drop to reach the harbour.

Things got a little easier after the steps were built, although the work was still backbreaking. Once the catch had been brought in, hardy local fisherwomen would gut and salt the fish, then pack them into heavy baskets to lug up the 365 steps. Their job wasn't done when they reached the cliff top, either; often they continued on foot to Wick, around 11 km (7 miles) away, from where most of the herring would be exported.

Today, the steps are open to visitors, although they can get very busy, especially in summer; come early or late to avoid the crowds, and keep noise to a minimum – the car park is right next to local houses. From here, you can make your way down the steps to the harbour area; the steps are steep and can be slippery in wet weather, so it pays to take it slow.

At the harbour, various items hark back to Whaligoe's glory days, including a winch to pull boats out of the water, a metal grill where a fire once heated tar (used to waterproof boats) and a salt store. It's a steep climb back up to the top, from where you can follow the John O'Groats Trail *(p86)* south to a view-point – it's just a five-minute stroll and the sight of the steps snaking up the cliff is truly impressive.

Despite the tests of time, the steps have remained in relatively good shape, even though some have been lost over the years (today there are only 337 left). This is in large part thanks to Davie Nicolson, the unofficial caretaker of the steps. Davie's dedication to Whaligoe is fuelled by a family tie: his grandfather used to sail from here in his boat, the *Morning Star*, and was one of the last fishers to use the harbour in the mid-20th century. For those who have the good fortune to bump into the moustachioed Davie (who is always found wearing his Harley-Davidson cap) expect to be treated to a wealth of stories about the steps. You might also be challenged to ride his "backwards bike"; with handlebars set up the wrong way (left is right and vice versa) and no brakes to speak of, it's a tricky contraption to get the hang of. Little wonder Davie has a tattoo on his left arm saying "Born to Raise Hell".

⓷⓼ Grey Cairns of Camster

///trees.socialite.kicks 🄰 Turn-off to cairns 2.5 km
(1.5 miles) north of Lybster, then another 8 km
(5 miles) along a single-track road to the cairns
🄿 Small car park on-site 🅦 historicenvironment.scot

Found along a remote single-track road inland from the Whaligoe Steps *(p74)*, these two stone cairns lie nestled amid the tawny landscapes of the Flow Country *(p100)*, a huge blanket bog. They're some of the oldest historical monuments in Scotland, built over 5,000 years ago by Neolithic peoples.

Wooden boardwalks lead from the car park to the cairns. To the north sits the long cairn, an undulating structure with two entrances leading to internal chambers. These once had corbelled dry-stone roofs, but they collapsed at some point, and so are now covered by fibreglass replacements.

Sandwiched in between Camster Cairns and Wick, **Puldagon Farm Shop and Restaurant** *(////mulls.smaller.postings; puldagonfarm.co.uk)* is run by husband-and-wife team Greg and Terri Hooker. It's situated on Greg's family farm, which dates back to 1925 and provides hyper-local produce for the restaurant, known for its generously filled burgers and (during autumn and winter) comforting Sunday lunches. Find other Highland goodies in the on-site shop.

Wander south to find the round cairn. Excavations during the 19th century revealed flint tools, pottery and burnt human remains within the chamber, as well as two skeletons in a separate area that had been blocked off. Archaeologists believe that the cairns were used as burial sites, although if this were the case, their location – in a dip without views of the sea or mountains – is unusual for the time period.

The inner chambers of the cairns can be explored; simply unlock the small metal gates in front of the entrance and clamber inside. Be warned, though: both the entrances and corridors are a very tight squeeze, especially in the round cairn. Once inside, it's a magical experience, with the ancient stone chambers lit by beams of natural light.

Clockwise from top left Strolling along the boardwalk to the cairns; the entrance to the round cairn; a chamber in the cairns, lit by sunlight; a narrow corridor inside one of the cairns

③⁹ Wick

Derived from the Old Norse word "Vik" (meaning bay), this settlement was founded by Vikings in the 12th century on the north side of the river. Towards the end of the 19th century, the British Fisheries Society built a new town – Pulteneytown – and harbour on the south side. Their intention was simple: to entice evicted crofters to the fishing industry. And the plan worked. By the 1860s, Wick was the world's busiest herring harbour, with around 1,100 boats in operation and roughly 85,000 barrels of salt fish produced every year. Many were exported, often to places as far afield as the West Indies, which is one of the reasons why salted fish is a key ingredient in many West Indian dishes, including Jamaica's national dish: saltfish and ackee.

The collapse of the herring industry led Wick to decline in importance. But while the town has a slightly down-at-heel feel, there's still plenty to explore in this sea-faring spot. First is the volunteer-run **Wick Heritage Centre**, which recounts the town's history, in particular its herring heyday. Exhibits include examples of fully rigged fishing boats and an old kippering kiln. There's the Johnston Photographic Collection, too: a series of images taken by three generations of a fishing family; they provide invaluable insight into local life. »

Wick Heritage Centre
///recapture.overgrown.undivided ⌂ 18–27 Bank Row
🅿 Public car parks close by 🕑 Easter–Oct: 10am–5pm
Mon–Sat; last entry 3.45pm 🆆 wickheritage.org 🔗

Right Walking towards the Trinkie, an old swimming pool south of Wick

A ten-minute walk from the heritage centre is **Old Pulteney Distillery**, set up in 1826 and named after the new town it was built in. Tours at this long-standing distillery take in everything from milling to maturation; the latter process, which sees the whisky stored in warehouses next to the harbourfront, accounts for the hint of sea salt that can be tasted in each dram. With such a connection to the sea, it's no wonder that the distillery has partnered with SeaTrees, a non-profit ocean initiative that helps protect, restore and regenerate blue ecosystems.

A short distance south of the town, the 15th-century **Castle of Old Wick** sits atop cliffs on a narrow promontory, its ruins dominated by a four-storey tower. Nearby is the **Trinkie**, a seaside lido dating from the 1930s. Plenty of locals have learned to swim here and it's still a nice place for a quick dip, although storms have caused some damage to the walls in recent years. There's also another historic lido, the **North Baths**, on the other side of Wick Bay.

For those looking to get a taste of life on the waves, **Caithness Seacoast** runs regular tours along the coast on RIBs (rigid inflatable boats). Set up by local skipper William Munro, who worked for almost 45 years in the merchant navy, the trips take in the area's spectacular coastal scenery, made up of miles of high cliffs dotted with sea stacks, caves and arches, and topped by crumbling castles. Expert tour guides delve into the geology and history of the area, and provide details on its wildlife: expect to see guillemots nesting in holes along the cliff face, northern gannets diving for fish and,

in the summer months, puffins resting on the sea's surface.

Old Pulteney Distillery
///rating.strictest.figure 🏠 Huddart Street
🅿 On-street parking on Huddart Street
🕐 10am–5pm Mon–Sat (Oct–Mar: to 4.30pm); check website for tour times (book ahead)
🔲 oldpulteney.com 🎟 🦽

Castle of Old Wick
///bleaching.diner.schematic 🅿 On-site, followed by 10-minute walk 🔲 historicenvironment.scot

Trinkie
///lush.defensive.cove 🏠 1.3 km (0.8 miles) from south end of Harbour Road 🅿 Small parking bay above lido

North Baths
///education.ballpoint.feasts 🏠 North side of the bay, just off The Shore 🅿 Camps car park, 10-minute walk from lido

Caithness Seacoast
///pens.grumbling.fairy 🏠 Harbour Road 🅿 On-site 🕐 Hours vary, check website 🔲 caithness-seacoast. co.uk 🎟 🦽

There are quite a few local, old-school pubs in Wick, but one of the best is **Mackays Bar** (////erupt.snuggle.lawful; mackayshotel. co.uk). It's in the popular Mackay's Hotel, which sits on Ebenezer Place – the shortest street in the world at 2.06 m (6 ft 9 in) long. The bar has an impressive collection of whiskies – over 500 types – including rare bottles from nearby Old Pulteney.

Clockwise from top left Guillemots perching on sea cliffs; William, the skipper and owner of Caithness Seacoast; an oystercatcher foraging along the shore; a sea arch spied from a RIB

❹ Castle Sinclair Girnigoe

///apart.safest.boldest 🏠 7 km (4.5 miles) from Wick
🅿 Noss Head Car Park

A short drive north of Wick *(p78)*, this late 15th-century castle sits dramatically on a narrow, sheer-sided sliver of rock surrounded on three sides by the sea. Such a location made it nearly impregnable, but its owners, Clan Sinclair, further improved its defensive position by building a dry moat in front of the main drawbridge.

Today, this once-formidable fortification has been reduced to ruins by a mixture of warfare and weather. Yet a sense of its original majesty still remains, thanks to its imposing 15th-century defensive wall and 16th-century tower house. Handy information panels next to the castle provide information on its history, as well as illustrations showing what it would have looked like at the height of its power. Sadly the interior of the castle is currently closed to visitors, due to the risk of falling masonry, but the Clan Sinclair Trust is committed to repairing it.

The castle sits on the northern flank of Noss Head, a large, nose-shaped peninsula – Noss comes from the old Norse "Snos", meaning "nose" – stretching out into the North Sea. This headland is home to a whole variety of wildlife, including short-eared owls and curlews. On its very tip sits Noss Head Lighthouse, from where you can glimpse Duncansby Head *(p84)* and, on a clear day, Orkney.

❹ Sinclairs Bay

///bubble.rides.perfumed 🅿 Public parking at Wick
Golf Club in Reiss, 6 km (4 miles) from Wick

Curving north from Castle Sinclair Girnigoe in a gentle crescent, this beautiful bay is divided into two separate beaches by the River Wester. To the south lies Reiss Sands, whose sheltered shores are popular with surfers, while to the north is Keiss Sands, watched over at its furthest end by the ruins of Old Keiss Castle. Both spots are sprinkled with a good helping of white, sugary sand and together stretch for almost 10 km (6 miles) – stroll beside them on the John O'Groats Trail *(p86)*.

There are several brochs (Iron Age dry-stone towers) nearby, including Nybster Broch and Ness Broch. See the **Caithness Broch Project** for more information.

Caithness Broch Project
🅦 thebrochproject.co.uk

Right The spectacular ruins of Castle Sinclair Girnigoe, perched above a natural harbour

⓸ Duncansby Head

///appealing.sprinkler.bulbs
🏠 Turn-off just before John O'Groats on the A99,
then 2.5 km (1.5 miles) along minor road
🅿 Duncansby Head Lighthouse

After Sinclairs Bay *(p82)*, the road reaches north through a mix of field and moor towards this rugged headland – mainland Britain's most northeasterly point.

From the car park next to the yellow-and-white Duncansby Lighthouse, trails weave south across the grassy moorland and along the cliff-lined coast, passing by remarkable rock formations. The first is the Geo of Scalites, a narrow inlet enclosed by sheer-sided cliffs. So many seabirds – such as fulmars, kittiwakes and guillemots – make their homes in this rocky crevice that it feels almost like looking at an apartment block for birds. Close up, the cacophony of bird calls can be deafening and the smell rather pungent.

The crowning glory of the headland are the famed Duncansby Head Sea Stacks, a duo of jagged rocks that rise out of the often churning sea. These 60-m- (200-ft-) high pyramidal peaks are thought to have been around for 6,000 years or so, their red sandstone whipped into shape over millennia by the wind, rain and waves. Just before the stacks is Thirle Door, a striking rock arch, while behind it lies mile upon mile of sheer cliffs. The John O'Groats Trail *(p86)* continues down the coast from here.

Left Looking towards Duncansby Head Sea Stacks, with Thirle Door in the foreground

❹ Bay of Sannick

///riper.harnessed.shears **P** Grassy car park off road, around 0.8 km (0.5 miles) west of Duncansby Head

Often bypassed by visitors racing to get to John O'Groats, this lovely pocket of white sand ringed by grass-covered dunes is simply stunning. The bay overlooks the Pentland Firth, the home of seals, seabirds and cetaceans like dolphins.

❹ John O'Groats

Just 2.5 km (1.5 miles) west of Duncansby Head (p84), scattered across flat grassy land on the edge of the Pentland Firth, is John O'Groats. This tiny village holds the title of mainland Britain's most northerly settlement and is also the end point of the famous Land's End to John O'Groats tour. These two facts account for the huge number of people visiting every year, all keen to take a photo next to its famous signpost (expect a swarm around it).

While it's true that the rest of the village is mostly a mix of souvenir shops and cafe-restaurants, there's still a couple of sights to explore. Expect excellent whisky tours at 8 **Doors Distillery**, great wildlife watching from the shore-line and some intriguing sculptures dotted along this stretch of coast. One of the best is *Nomadic Boulders*, found just opposite the John O'Groats signpost. Made up of several huge rocks balanced on a series of arching metal beams, it is an homage to the power of the Pentland Firth, whose ferocious currents – feared by local sailors – are strong enough to move huge boulders vast distances along the ocean floor.

The village is also the starting point of the **John O'Groats Trail**, often mentioned in this chapter. Running all the way to Inverness, the 237-km (147-mile) route is still a work in progress (some sections are pathless) but the beauty of the east coast – towering cliffs, sandy shorelines, rocky bays – is guaranteed.

8 Doors Distillery
///pods.drifting.quite 🏠 Next to main car park **P** Just outside building 🕐 Hours vary, check website for times, including tours **W** 8doorsdistillery.com

John O'Groats Trail
W jogt.org.uk

The biggest selling point of John O'Groats' **Together Travel Lodges** (///outhouse.headstone.tips; togethertravel.co.uk)? The stunning views out across the Pentland Firth. There are two types of accommodation to choose from: cosy lodges with wood-burning stoves or charming apartments in the restored 19th-century inn, instantly recognizable thanks to its colourful Scandi-style extension.

Clockwise from top The colourful apartments of Together Travel Lodges;
looking over the sea from the village; John O'Groats' much-visited signpost

87

NORTH COAST

Start John O'Groats

≫

End Durness

Left Grassy sand dunes backing
the beautiful Balnakeil Beach

NORTH COAST

From John O'Groats, the route unspools along Scotland's remote northern coastline, the landscape transforming from neat fields of arable farmland to moody moorland punctuated by the looming peaks of bens Hope and Loyal. The road, too, changes as you travel further west, with two-way lanes shrinking down into narrow single-tracks after expansive Loch Eriboll – something that makes for trickier, yet more interesting, driving. And as for sights? Sandy beaches come thick and fast after Thurso; rugged, bird-cloaked headlands jut out from the coastline; and several spots speak to the brutal Clearances that happened across the Highlands, whether it's abandoned townships like Ceannabeinne or Bettyhill's thought-provoking Strathnaver Museum. Suffice to say, this stretch is not one to rush, so make sure to slow down and take it all in.

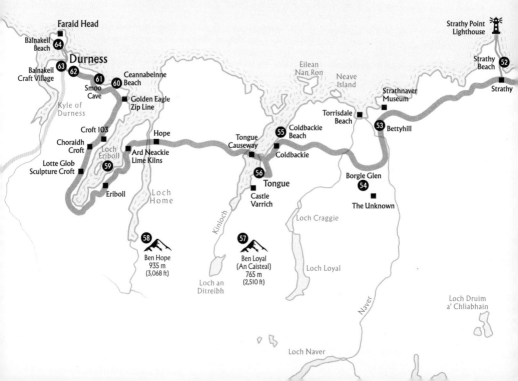

Faraid Head

Balnakeil Beach **64**

Durness

Balnakeil Craft Village **63** **62**

61

60 Ceannabeinne Beach

Smoo Cave

Golden Eagle Zip Line

Kyle of Durness

Croft 103

Choraidh Croft

Hope

Loch Eriboll

Lotte Glob Sculpture Croft

Ard Neackie Lime Kilns

59

Eriboll

Loch Home

Tongue Causeway

Coldbackie

Castle Varrich

56

Tongue

Kinloch

58 Ben Hope 935 m (3,068 ft)

57 Ben Loyal (An Caisteal) 765 m (2,510 ft)

Loch an Ditreibh

Loch Craggie

Loch Loyal

Eilean Nan Ron

Neave Island

Strathnaver Museum

Torrisdale Beach

Coldbackie Beach **55**

Borgie Glen **54**

The Unknown

53 Bettyhill

Strathy Point Lighthouse

Strathy Beach **52**

Strathy

Naver

Loch Druim a' Chliabhain

Loch Naver

Orkney Islands

Hoy

Fara

Flotta

ATLANTIC

OCEAN

Pentland Firth

Stroma

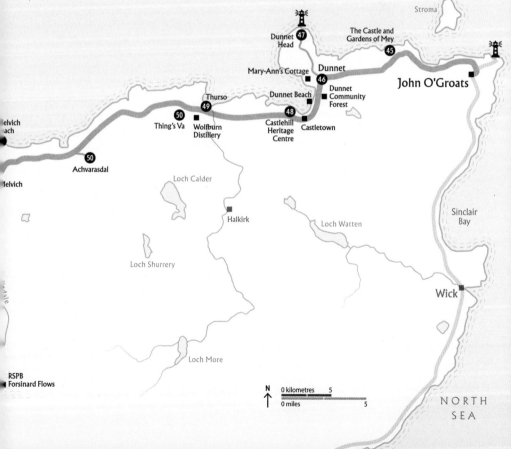

Dunnet
Head

47

The Castle and
Gardens of Mey

45

Mary-Ann's Cottage

Dunnet

46

John O'Groats

Dunnet Beach

Thurso

49

Dunnet
Community
Forest

Thing's Va

Wolfburn
Distillery

48

Castlehill
Heritage
Centre

Castletown

Ielvich
ach

50

Achvarasdal

50

Loch Calder

Ielvich

Halkirk

Loch Watten

Sinclair
Bay

Loch Shurrery

Wick

Loch More

RSPB
Forsinard Flows

N

0 kilometres   5

0 miles   5

NORTH
SEA

ⓐ The Castle and Gardens of Mey

///alert.snug.blues 🏠 Around 11 km (7 miles) west of John O'Groats,
see signposted turning off the A836 🅿 On-site 🕐 May–Sep: castle: 11am–3pm (last entry)
Wed–Sun; gardens and grounds: 10.30am–4pm Wed–Sun 🆆 castleofmey.org.uk 🧭

From John O'Groats the route heads west, charting a course along the coast to the Castle and Gardens of Mey. This turreted castle, set amid a patchwork of green fields, was the seat of the earls of Caithness for over 300 years. Yet it's most famous for being the summer retreat of Queen Elizabeth, the Queen Mother, who bought it in a state of disrepair in 1952 following the death of her husband, King George VI. She renovated the house, bringing it back to its former glory and filling it with beloved possessions, including a number of artworks by her grandson, now King Charles III; many of these can be seen on a tour through the castle's picturesque rooms today.

The royal family still holiday here for several weeks each summer, lured by the beautiful views across the Pentland Firth towards Orkney – the castle is just a short distance from the shore.

To the east of the castle is a beautiful walled garden, protected from salt spray and high winds by the 3.5-m (12-ft) Great Wall of Mey. It's filled with rhododendrons, fuchsias and other pretty blooms, as well as some vegetables (many of which get put to good use in the on-site tearoom). To the west, meanwhile, lie fields of sheep and an Animal Centre, home to a host of creatures including Buff Orpingtons, a regal breed of chicken once kept by the Queen Mother.

Clockwise from top The regal exterior of the Castle of Mey; looking towards the garden's greenhouses; a selection of the beautiful plants inside the garden

Clockwise from top left Holy grass, one of the ingredients used at Dunnet Bay Distillers; lemon thyme, another of the ingredients used; sampling some spirits; Kolin King, a member of the team, showcasing the geodome

⁴⁶ Dunnet

Leaving the Castle of Mey *(p92)*, the route makes an almost straight shot through farmland for Dunnet. Barely more than a couple of streets, this tiny village has more going for it than you'd initially think, and the first stop on any tour should be **Dunnet Bay Distillers**. Set up by husband-and-wife team Martin and Claire Murray, the distillery is famous for its award-winning Rock Rose gin, as well as its focus on local ingredients. Most of the components of its gins are sourced from the surrounding landscape, from the sea buckthorn hand-foraged from nearby Dunnet Community Forest to the rock rose root sourced from the cliffs of the Pentland Firth. The distillery has its own garden, too, complete with a geodome greenhouse, where it grows many of its own botanicals.

Tours cover the distillery's gin- and vodka-making processes, taking in the shining copper stills, one of which is called Elizabeth after the Castle of Mey's very own Queen Mother. Keep an eye out in the stills room for the shelves of bottles containing experimental batches (smiley faces are used to note which ones will make the cut). And if you're really lucky, Mr Mackintosh – Claire and Martin's dog and unofficial distillery apprentice – will join you on your tour. He's easy to spot thanks to the red bandana always tied around his neck.

Beyond the distillery, there's excellent walking at **Dunnet Community Forest**, which on Thursdays and Sundays welcomes "green gym" volunteers who help keep the forest healthy – check out its website for more information on getting involved. The village also sits at the north end of Dunnet Beach, a wide arc of white sand that's bordered by huge grassy dunes. It's a great spot for surfing, with lessons offered by Iona and Finn, both ex-members of Scotland's national surf team and now owners of **North Coast Watersports**.

Dunnet's final attraction is **Mary-Ann's Cottage**, a mid-19th-century building that gives a taste of how Caithness crofters once lived. Alongside the original furniture and historic tools and machinery, there are a number of repurposed objects, evidence of the crofter's need for a thrifty attitude.

Dunnet Bay Distillers
///lawfully.actors.magic ⌂ Signposted turning off the A836 in Dunnet 🅿 On-site; EV charging available 🕐 10am–5pm Mon–Sat (Nov–Mar: to 4pm); check website for tour times Ⓦ dunnetbaydistillers.co.uk 🪪 🅖

Dunnet Community Forest
///paradise.dance.column ⌂ 1.6 km (1 mile) south of Dunnet; signposted turning off the A836 for Dunnet Forest Walks 🅿 On-site Ⓦ dunnetcommunityforest.org

North Coast Watersports
Ⓦ northcoastwatersports.com

Mary-Ann's Cottage
///repeat.salutes.crusted ⌂ Ness Road 🅿 On-site 🕐 Hours vary, check website Ⓦ maryannscottage.org 🪪 🅖

❼ Dunnet Head

///await.sank.widen 🅰 Around 24 km (15 miles)
west of John O'Groats, see signposted turning off the
A836 🅿 On-site, just before lighthouse 🅦 rspb.org.uk

Despite what many may think, Dunnet
Head is the most northerly point of
Britain (not the more famous John
O'Groats to the east). Bulging north of
the small town of Dunnet *(p94)*, its tip
is topped by yet another Stevenson-made
lighthouse, which warns boats of the high
cliffs below. But while these sheer walls
have been avoided by sailors old and new,
they're a regular hangout for all kinds of
seabirds. In fact, during the spring and
summer, the cliff face at this RSPB-
protected nature reserve comes alive with
nesting birds, including "bawkies" and
"molly-mawks" (local Caithness slang for
razorbills and fulmars). Expect to see
puffins, too, referred to as "tammie
norries" by the folks in Orkney, just across
the Pentland Firth.

Several paths lead from Dunnet Head
car park across the headland. Choose
the trail running south for excellent
bird-watching or walk east to a stellar
viewpoint, which has panoramic vistas
across to Orkney, Duncansby Head
and, on a good day, even as far as Cape
Wrath *(p126)*. Be sure to take notice of
the ground beneath your feet, too.
The moorland provides habitat for a
range of beautiful plants. Among them
are spring squill, which blooms with
tiny blue flowers from March to April,
and sea campion, whose fleshy leaves
stop the plant from drying out in the
salty air.

Top left Puffins nesting along the cliff face
Bottom left A seal bobbing in the waters below the headland
Above The high cliffs of Dunnet Head, topped by a lighthouse

🔵48 Castlehill Heritage Centre

///ritual.chatters.romantics 🏠 Harbour Road, Castletown 🅿 On-site 🕐 2pm–4pm Wed, Sat & Sun 🌐 castletownheritage.co.uk 💲 Donation

At the southern end of Dunnet Beach (p95) is Castletown, a simple settlement that was once a hub of commercial flagstone production. The story of this industry is told at the village's Castlehill Heritage Centre, which is housed in an old steading located next to the quarry and cutting yard of the former flagstone workings. The centre also touches on other important parts of the village's history, such as the impact of Viking habitation and the role Castletown played in the defence of British waters during World War II.

Thanks to a lack of light pollution, this spot is also a Dark Sky Discovery Site; on a clear night expect incredible views of the star-strewn heavens above.

🔵49 Thurso

From Castletown, the A836 stretches straight as an arrow through more coastal farmland, before winding its way through Thurso. Taking its name from the Norse "Thorsa", meaning "Thor's River", this town was once an important Viking settlement, although most of its stately grey-sandstone buildings date from the Victorian period. For many travellers on the North Coast 500, Thurso is simply a stopping point to pick up supplies (it's the last big town before Ullapool (p150) or is bypassed completely in the rush to reach the nearby port of Scrabster, where ferries depart to Orkney and its world-famous collection of Neolithic sites.

But those in the know tend to linger a little longer here, not least to explore the **North Coast Visitor Centre**, a cultural one-stop-shop housed in the old town hall. Inside, an artifact-packed museum traces Thurso's history, touching on the area's geology, inhabitants such as the Picts and Vikings, and its links to Dounreay nuclear power plant. Elsewhere, there's a gallery showcasing works by local artists and a theatre offering a changing programme of performances.

From the centre, a short walk to the west leads to **Thurso Beach**, a pleasant strip of sand, while east takes you to the ruins of **Old St Peter's Church**, the town's oldest building at over 800 years old. Across the river from the latter is Thurso East, a point break that's popular with experienced surfers for its impressive barrel waves; those looking for gentler surf should try the beaches at Dunnet (p95), Melvich (p100) or Bettyhill (p105).

Just outside of Thurso proper is **Wolfburn Distillery**. First established in the 1820s, it fell into disrepair for over 100 years, but was brought back to life in 2012. As with the whisky makers of the past, today's distillers use the clear waters of the nearby Wolf Burn (hence the distillery's name) to create their award-winning whiskies. Indeed, the team here takes a hands-on approach – everything from the milling to the bottling is done by hand – giving Wolfburn a personal, down-to-earth feel that some of its more polished contemporaries lack. Tours, as you'd expect, cover the whisky-making process and include tastings.

North Coast Visitor Centre

///text.enclosing.estuaries 🏠 High Street, Thurso 🅿 Public parking across from the entrance; several other car parks within walking distance, including on the main street, but these have time restrictions 🕒 Hours vary, check website 🅦 highlifehighland.com/north-coast-visitor-centre 🔁 Donation

Thurso Beach

///absorb.shift.fallback 🏠 Pentland Crescent 🅿 On-site at Pentland Crescent car park

Old St Peter's Church

///scanning.audit.insulated 🏠 Wilson Lane, Thurso 🅿 Pentland Crescent car park, then short walk

Wolfburn Distillery

///haggling.playing.postage 🏠 Henderson Park, Thurso 🅿 On-site 🕒 Hours vary, check website 🅦 wolfburn.com 🔁 🖿

The name of **Thurso Community Cafe** (///pats.shiny.clinic; thursocommunity cafe.co.uk) says it all. This laid-back spot, housed in an old stone building in the town centre, is all about engaging and supporting the local community, whether through its games room, community larder or variety of support groups. The cafe is excellent, serving up coffee, cakes and a warm welcome.

⑤⓪ Thing's Va and Achvarasdal

Scattered across the Caithness landscape are a large number of brochs, soaring drystone towers built by Iron Age communities. Although the purpose of these prehistoric structures has been debated, today archaeologists believe that they were used as communal dwellings, with everything from crafting to sleeping carried out within their walls.

Several brochs lie a stone's throw west of Thurso, including Thing's Va. Built roughly 2,000 years ago, its name is believed to derive from Thing's Vollr, Norse for a parliament, suggesting that the Vikings reused the broch as a meeting place to discuss important matters. Little remains apart from indentations in the grassy landscape, but it still has a compelling atmosphere, one enhanced by the excellent views across the Pentland Firth.

Another nearby broch is Achvarasdal, one of the best-preserved and well-looked-after brochs in the area, with one of the largest diameters at around 10 m (33 ft). It can be reached on a short loop walk through regenerating woodland.

Thing's Va

///beaten.saved.jaundice 🏠 Around 5 km (3 miles) west of Thurso, see signposted turning for Hill of Forss off the A836 🅿 Large opening on right, 1 km (0.6 miles) after turning for Hill of Forss 🅦 thebrochproject.co.uk

Achvarasdal

///unfolds.dice.screen 🏠 See signposted turning off the A836 🅿 In layby near entrance 🅦 thebrochproject.co.uk

⑤ Melvich Beach

///clinking.aced.outreach 🏠 See signposted turning off the A836 🅿 Northwest of the beach, follow signs

Following the road west through a mix of fertile fields and rugged, heather-sprinkled moorland, the North Coast 500 skirts close to Melvich Beach. This spread of golden sand stretches from the rocky headlands beneath the tiny hamlet of Portskerra to the edge of the glimmering River Halladale, which curves gently around the narrow spit of land on which the beach sits. The blue-green waters here are popular with swimmers and surfers year-round, while in spring the dunes that back the beach are liberally daubed with bright-yellow cowslips.

Enshrouding great swathes of Caithness and Sutherland, RSPB Forsinard Flows is the largest blanket bog in the world. The peaty landscape, which was named a World Heritage Site by UNESCO in 2024, provides a habitat for rare wildlife and holds vast amounts of carbon, making it important both for protecting biodiversity and in the fight against climate change. The RSPB Forsinard Flows Visitor Centre, 25 km (15.5 miles) south of Melvich Beach in the local train station, is a great place to learn more about the bog. From here, a series of boardwalks lead to a viewing tower, where you can take in the mossy, pond-dotted terrain from on high.

⑤ Strathy Beach

///nesting.richer.patrolled 🏠 See signposted turning for Strathy East Beach (if coming from east) or Strathy West Beach (if coming from west), just off the A836 🅿 Strathy Cemetery Parking

Beautiful beaches come thick and fast on the north coast, with Strathy next on the list. This wide pocket of golden sand is bordered by small cliffs to the east, grassy dunes to the south and the River Strathy to the west. The path to the beach winds steeply down the dunes, which in May and June are peppered with northern marsh orchids and spring squills. Though the soft sands are often quiet, expect to see a few surfers, who come to take advantage of the sheltered bay.

West of the bay, a bumpy, single-track road runs along Strathy Point. At the end is Strathy Point Lighthouse, from where there are beautiful views along the rolling, rocky coastline in both directions, including east back across the beach.

Above The golden sands of Strathy Beach,
one of the north coast's many beautiful beaches

❸ Bettyhill

Nestled amid green hills and overlooking the sea, this small crofting village packs a punch, largely thanks to the fascinating **Strathnaver Museum**. Housed in an 18th-century church, this largely volunteer-run spot recounts the history of the area, with special focus on the Highland Clearances and their aftermath. During the early 19th century, locals were removed from their homes by the Duke of Sutherland to make way for large-scale sheep farms. While this happened across the Highlands, the forced evictions in this area and the rest of Sutherland were particularly violent. Afterwards, these displaced communities were forced to make new lives along the coast, setting up settlements like Bettyhill and turning to industries such as lime production, kelp harvesting and fishing; others left Scotland entirely, emigrating to places like America. Many objects on display have been donated by locals, so the

collection and the story it tells feels very much rooted in the community.

The museum also showcases artifacts from the area's early inhabitants, including a Bronze-Age burial beaker by the Beaker People, and has several important archaeological sites in its graveyard, among them the Farr Stone, a 9th-century Pictish gravestone. Close by is the museum's annex, a wooden-clad building home to a display of agricultural and fishing items, and a gallery space for temporary exhibitions. »

Running south from Bettyhill, the 40-km (25-mile) Strathnaver Trail starts at Strathnaver Museum and takes in a total of 29 history-focused sights, including Neolithic and Bronze Age cairns, Iron Age brochs, and now-ruined townships, such as Rosal, which were left deserted following the Clearances. Key stops on the driving route include the stone circle of Clach An Righ and the atmospheric Coille na Borgie horned chamber cairns.

Strathnaver Museum
///hydration.clings.divisible 🏠 Clachan, Bettyhill
🅿 Next to the Clachan Cafe 🆆 strathnavermuseum.org.uk 🎴 🎴 Offered via Smartify

Above left A beaker made by the Beaker People

Above The excellent Strathnaver Museum, housed in an old church

Clockwise from top Joanna Mackenzie (left), the owner of The Store Cafe,
and Hellie Tarrant (right), the chef; a sign for cakes; the exterior of the cafe
Right Customers sitting inside the cosy cafe

Not far from the museum is the stunning **Farr Beach**, a crescent of pale gold sand found northwest of the village. Surfing is a possibility here, as is a good – if often bracing – walk along the coast to a viewpoint overlooking the bay and on towards the remains of Borve Castle. There's not much left to see of the latter, but the headland it once stood on is the site of a striking sea arch and the coastal views are very pretty.

Bettyhill also overlooks **Torrisdale Beach**, but it's not possible to access it from the village. Instead, you'll need to take a short 1.5-km (0.9-mile) walk from Invernaver, just west. This beautiful beach follows the Naver River towards the sea, before tracking the edge of the coast west in a sprawl of golden sand. There's history in abundance: the ruins of Druim Chuibhe, an Iron Age broch, sit atop the hill overlooking the beach, while at low tide, the rusted remains of the *SS John Randolph*, a ship sunk by Allied minefields during World War II, reveals itself. As at Farr, surfers come here to try their luck, too.

Farr Beach
///coasting.wisely.discussed 🏠 Bettyhill
🅿 Outside Bettyhill Tourist Information

Torrisdale Beach
///puzzle.centrally.soup 🏠 Invernaver
🅿 Parking area off the A836, just east of the bridge over the River Naver; note there's little parking available in Invernaver itself

The Store Cafe (///*stockpile.flattens.moves*; *storecafe.co.uk*) is Bettyhill's beating heart. It's run by Joanna Mackenzie, who first opened a laundry business in the village's old general store, with a comfy sofa and coffee machine. On opening day, keen villagers arrived looking for a hangout – and The Store Cafe was born. Now, it's a social hub providing a warm welcome and tasty food, with custom from road trippers helping to support the cafe off-season. It's also fulfilled a promise Joanna made to her mum: that she'd build a cafe at the end of their garden (the family home sits just behind). A must-visit.

❺❹ Borgie Glen

///archives.cosmic.define 🏠 10 km (6 miles) southwest
of Bettyhill, see signposted turning for Borgie Glen
🅿 Around 1 km (0.5 miles) after turning for Borgie
Glen 🆆 forestryandland.gov.scot/visit/borgie-glen

South of Torrisdale Beach, the road heads
inland to Borgie Glen, a forested area cut
through by paths and mountain-biking
routes. Many of the paths aren't waymarked, so bring a compass and map.

One of the paths that is signposted,
however, leads to a surprising sight: a
rusted-iron skeleton. Perched on a
rocky knoll, this strangely forlorn figure
looks out over forest- and heather-clad
moorland towards Ben Hope and Ben
Loyal *(p108)*. Named *The Unknown*,
it was created by acclaimed artist Kenny
Hunter – better known for his civic works
– and represents an outcast, drawing
on themes of exile in Scottish history,
including the Highland Clearances *(p102)*.
It also links back to local folklore, where
stories of giants loom large; in one tale,
two behemoths launched boulders at each
other between Bettyhill and Skerray.

❺❺ Coldbackie Beach

///basically.spines.initiated 🏠 Coldbackie 🅿 Layby on
edge of the A836, then steep walk down to beach

Yet another stunning beach on the north
coast, Coldbackie's silky white sands are
backed by sand dunes and fronted by
twinkling waters. It's a bit of a steep hike
to get down to the beach, but that means
it's often deserted – apart from a handful

Rather than crossing the Kyle of Tongue via
the causeway, a 14.5-km (9-mile) detour loops
around the edge of the Kyle instead. From
Tongue, a single-track road winds down the
sea loch's eastern side to the mouth of the
Kinloch River, before wiggling its way up the
western edge to emerge near the end of the
causeway. On the way are the mountains
of Ben Hope and Ben Loyal *(p108)*, the
lochans of Hakon and na Cuilce, and the
ruins of Dùn Mhaigh, an Iron Age broch.

of surfers who come to glide over the waves
when there's an Atlantic swell. From the
beach, there are views across to velvety
green Rabbit Islands, once home to many
of these long-eared animals, and Orkney.

❺❻ Tongue

Clustered on the eastern side of the Kyle
of Tongue, this settlement is little more
than a collection of houses grouped around
the Tongue Hotel. Its main attraction is
Castle Varrich, a stocky ruin that watches
over the village from atop a grassy hill.
Thought to have been built 1,000 years
ago, it was once the medieval stronghold
of the Mackays, the clan who dominated
much of the area. The 2.5-km (1.5-mile)
path up to the castle passes through young
woodland by the river, before snaking
upwards through broom and heather.
Inside the castle, a freestanding staircase
has been erected, providing excellent
views of Ben Loyal *(p108)* and the Kyle
of Tongue.

Above View towards the Kyle of Tongue Causeway
from the village of Tongue

Upon leaving Tongue, the route heads over the Kyle via the Tongue Causeway. If crossing at high tide, it almost feels as though you're gliding upon the sea itself, while at low tide golden-hued sand flats appear on either side – prime feeding ground for wading birds. A car park on the causeway provides the perfect chance to pull in and admire the view over the sea loch, with the high peaks of Ben Loyal and Ben Hope *(p108)* rising to the south. There's also an information point covering the geological history of the area.

From the western end of the causeway, a right turn off the route snakes along a dead-end road, past several pretty beaches, including those at Achininver and Talmine. The Countryside Rangers *(p15)* sometimes offer guided nature walks from the former.

The plush **Tongue Hotel** *(///views.flopped. crispier; tonguehotel.co.uk)* is a welcome sight after a day on the road. Expect cosy rooms with comfortable beds, complimentary whisky and decor reflecting the colours of the surrounding landscape. To top it off, the on-site restaurant is top notch (the Scottish breakfast will keep you going for days).

Castle Varrich
///clean.logbook.cabbage 🏠 Tongue
🅿 Public parking opposite the Ben Loyal Hotel

⑤⑦ Ben Loyal

///incisions.snipe.slamming 🅿 Small parking area
at Rigbill, 3 km (2 miles) south of Tongue

South of Tongue, this impressive 765-m
(2,510-ft) Corbett is actually made up
of four separate peaks, helping to give it
the moniker of the "Queen of Scottish
Mountains". An Caisteal is the highest
of the quartet and is reached by a rather
boggy and unmarked climb (it's not one
for inexperienced hikers). The views
from the top are incredible, taking in
lochan-dotted Flow Country *(p100)*,
surrounding mountain peaks and the
tidal Kyle of Tongue.

⑤⑧ Ben Hope

///values.basically.candy 🅿 Signposted turning for
Altnaharra off the A838; parking on left, 3 km
(2 miles) south of head of Loch Hope; path
begins with a "way up Ben Hope" sign

About 26 km (16 miles) southwest of
Tongue is the isolated peak of Ben Hope,
Scotland's most northerly Munro, which
rises high above the area's blanket bog.
The route to the top is clearly waymarked,
but it's a steep climb, with the 935 m
(3,068 ft) to the summit covered in just
4.5 km (2.8 miles). As with Ben Loyal,
there are perfect panoramas from its
peak, including of the Strathmore River
making its way into inky-blue Loch Hope.

Right Ben Loyal's quartet of peaks,
seen across the Kyle of Tongue

59 Loch Eriboll

The North Coast 500 winds around this glittering loch, which is lined on three sides by grassy hills and brooding mountains; the fourth side to the north connects with the wild and blustery Atlantic. Loch Eriboll is one of Scotland's deepest, stretching down to 60 m (197 ft) in places, and is also an important geo-logical site. Limestone makes up its eastern side, quartzite its western side, evidence of when Scotland was two separate continents.

The loch's best-known site is the **Ard Neackie Lime Kilns**, four well-preserved kilns perched on a tiny, anvil-shaped headland. Dating from around 1870, these stone ovens once produced copious amounts of quicklime, used in both building works and agriculture. Today, you can wander across to the headland – connected to the mainland by a thin, sandy strip of land – to admire the remains of the kilns. From the arched exterior, a rough track leads to the shafts at the top of the kilns (be careful, they're deep), before continuing on to a now-flooded quarry. The building near to the kilns was once the home of ferry keepers, who ran boats across the loch until the 1890s.

On the opposite side of the loch lies the **Lotte Glob Sculpture Croft**. Set up by Danish ceramicist Lotte Glob, who has lived on the north coast of Scotland for 50 years, the Sculpture Croft com-prises 14 acres of land dotted with many of Lotte's striking abstract sculptures. There's a studio, too, where Lotte can often be found working on her next project.

Ard Neackie Lime Kilns
///flopping.masterpiece.pins 🅰 Heilam
🅿 There's a small parking bay just off the main road, from where you can follow a single-track road down to the kilns

Lotte Glob Sculpture Croft
///skill.imported.bulge 🅰 105 Laid 🅿 On-site

On the loch's western edge, the **Choraidh Croft** (///souk.shunted.stooping; choraidhcroft.co.uk) is home to an excellent caravan park that offers stunning views over the loch and surrounding hills. You'll need to be a Caravan & Motorhome Club Member to stay here, but no worries if not – there's also a cosy tearoom and cute craft shop to explore.

Croft 103 (///quail.crowbar.dolls; croft103.com) is all about eco-friendly living. Its two zero-carbon, self-catering cottages were built to be as low-impact as possible, with electricity coming from a wind turbine and heating via solar collectors. Designed using traditional techniques, the buildings were constructed from local stone, timber and sheep's wool (the latter was used for insulation).

Left A striking headland on Loch Eriboll, on which sit the Ard Neackie Lime Kilns

⑥ Ceannabeinne Beach

///herbs.broadens.thick ⌂ 40 km (25 miles) from
Tongue 🅿 Car park just off the A838, with path on
opposite side of road

Much of the route around Loch Eriboll
(p110) is along meandering single-track
roads, so it's eventually a relief to leave the
loch behind and reach Ceannabeinne Beach.
Overlooked by rocky Beinn Ceannabeinne,
which stands at 383 m (1,257 ft) high, this
stretch of white, sugary sand enclosed by
pale waters looks surprisingly tropical for
the far north of Scotland – at least on a
sunny day. A short trail down the side of
a grassy hill leads to the beach, which is
surrounded by pink-hued cliffs and has
excellent views of emerald Eilean Hoan
island, a nature reserve. According to
legend, the beach was where a local lady
was found dead after falling in the river;
this accounts for its Gaelic name Traigh
Alt Chailgeag ("The beach of the burn
of bereavement and death"), a sombre
moniker that sits in stark contrast to the
beauty of this spot.

Thanks to its sheltered position, the
beach is a nice place for a relaxed dip,
but those looking for something more
adrenaline-fuelled should try the **Golden
Eagle Zipline**. Sitting 100 ft (30 m) above
the beach, it reaches speeds of 72 km/h
(45 mph) while offering stunning views of
the sandy shore and beyond.

To the east and west of the beach are two
more perfect pockets of sand, Rispond and
Sangobeg, which are often much quieter
than Ceannabeinne. The Ceannabeinne
Township Trail is also nearby; offering
coastal panoramas, this short walk winds
around a now-ruined village that was abandoned during the Clearances. The information boards provide interesting facts about
the site's history. See WalkHighlands *(p15)*
for more information.

Golden Eagle Zipline
🕐 Weather dependant, turn up on the day
🌐 durnesszipline.com 🔀

Above A hill above Ceannabeinne dotted with glacial erratics
Right The beautiful beach itself

⑥ Smoo Cave

///curly.kite.clay ⬆ Signposted off the A838 🅿 On-site, next to public toilets 🕒 24 hrs daily

Part of the Northwest Highlands Geopark *(p130)*, this vast sea cave is deservedly one of the most popular sights on the route. Situated at the end of a narrow inlet, Smoo – whose name comes from the Old Norse "Smúga", meaning cave – was formed over thousands of years by the dual forces of river and sea.

While the elements created the cave, humans have long seen it as a place of refuge. In fact, archaeologists believe that the cave was used by the area's first hunter-gatherers, who arrived in Scotland around 7,000 years ago; evidence of their presence is seen in a shell midden next to the cave's entrance. These early peoples were followed by Vikings, for whom the cave was used as a base for fishing and boat building, with ship nails and rivets found during excavations.

To explore the cave on foot, take the path to the east of the car park, which offers striking views of Smoo's gaping mouth – it's one of the largest entrances in Great Britain. Inside, the cave opens up into a huge cathedral-like chamber complete with an eye-shaped window in the roof. From here, a covered walkway leads into a separate section with a tinkling waterfall. For those eager to explore the cave further by water, **Smoo Cave Tours** is the only operator to run trips.

Smoo Cave Tours
🕒 Hours vary, check website
W smoocavetours.com 🟦 🟦

Above The huge entrance to Smoo Cave,
one of the biggest cave entrances in Great Britain

⁶² Durness

Scattered across lush farmland, this loose collection of houses certainly feels remote, and no wonder, as this is the most north-westerly village on mainland Scotland. Slightly surprisingly, this spot has ties to the Beatles' John Lennon, who visited family here during childhood. There's a memorial to him outside the village hall.

The biggest draw in Durness is the beautiful beach, which is divided into three sections by rocky outcrops. It can get busy during the summer months – especially when the excellent Sango Sands Oasis campsite to the south is in full swing – but tends to be much quieter outside of the high season. A viewpoint just north of the campsite offers a bird's-eye view of the beach, whose sand owes its dusky pink colour to the area's Lewisian gneiss rock, formed around 2.5 million years ago. Thanks to the beach's relatively sheltered location, it's also popular for surfing and wild swimming, as well as walking.

Perched above Durness Beach in a humble car park is **Cheese 'N' Toasted** (///walkway.mirroring.misted), a powder-blue food truck serving generously sized toasties. There are plenty of options to choose from, including the pizza toastie (pepperoni and Italian herbs) and the Highlander (haggis and peppercorn sauce). Whichever you choose, it'll also come packed with three different types of gooey cheese, so take a napkin when it's offered – you'll need it.

⁶³ Balnakeil Craft Village

///bibs.enough.dine ⬆ Around 1 km (0.5 miles) west of Durness; follow signposted turning to Cocoa Mountain 🅿 On-site 🕓 Hours vary, check website for opening times of individual sights 🌐 balnakeilcraftvillage.weebly.com

In terms of surprising origin stories on the North Coast 500, this spot takes the biscuit. The village started life in the 1950s as an early warning station for the Ministry of Defence, which was concerned about a Cold War nuclear attack on British soil. Such an event failed to come to pass and so, in the 1960s, the local council initiated the Far North Project – essentially an attempt to lure artists and crafters to live at the site and set up creative businesses. People from across the UK applied and in no time at all, the Balnakeil Craft Village was born.

Fast-forward to today and the village – which still has a hippie-esque air – is owned and run by its residents. It's made up of an eclectic mix of spots, including several art galleries, a pottery and a boat repair workshop. Top of the list, though, has to be Deep Time, a museum on the fascinating geology of Durness that's run by Dr Björn S Hardarson, who sometimes offers geology-focused walks around the area. And no one should leave without visiting Cocoa Mountain. Started as a hobby by James Findlay and Paul Maden in the early 2000s, this first-class chocolatier makes for an excellent pitstop thanks to its delectable handmade truffles and world-famous hot chocolate.

Clockwise from top left A selection of truffles at Cocoa Mountain; a hot chocolate being prepared; one of the hot chocolates in a mug; James Findlay, co-founder of the chocolatier

⟨64⟩ Balnakeil Beach and Faraid Head

///enchanted.foods.richer 🏠 Around 1.6 km (1 mile) west of Durness, past Balnakeil Craft Village
🅿 In front of Balnakeil Church

Less than 1 km (0.6 miles) from the craft village *(p116)* is Balnakeil Beach, one of the most beautiful beaches on the whole route – and that's saying something. Hugging the western edge of a rugged peninsula, its pale white sands curve in a gentle arc around an emerald-blue bay. At high tide, when the waters shimmy up the sand, a rocky outcrop positioned in the middle of the beach neatly divides it into two; when the tide is low, the beach is one long 3-km (2-mile) stretch.

As it faces west, Balnakeil Beach is a great place to catch the sunset, as well as being a prime spot to watch birds like ringed plovers, who attempt to lure would-be predators away from their nests by dashing across the shore. Oystercatchers – instantly recognizable thanks to their orange beaks – are also a regular feature.

High dunes rise behind the beach, covered in thick clumps of bushy marram grass that help to prevent erosion. Despite this grassy blanket, the dunes are easily damaged, so it's best not to cycle on or slide down the slopes. This is especially important as the dunes are a Special Site of Scientific Interest (SSSI), providing a habitat for the likes of sand martins who build their nests in the sandy banks. The »

Right Looking out over Balnakeil Beach from atop sandy dunes

area is also used for local livestock, so don't be surprised if you see groups of cows or sheep ambling among the sandy hills (remember to keep dogs on a lead, especially during lambing season).

From the dunes, a stroll north leads out to Faraid Head, a horned headland that flares out into the iron-grey waters of the Atlantic. Here the landscape changes from soft sand and rolling dunes to windswept coastal heathland, which is dotted with wildflowers come spring and summer. During these seasons, the headland is an excellent spot to spy seabirds – among them fulmars, shags and puffins – who come to nest on the rocky cliffs and sea stacks, feeding their young from the surrounding waters. The seas here are also a prime spot to glimpse a variety of marine mammals, from often ubiquitous seals to more elusive denizens of the deep like bottlenose dolphins, harbour porpoises and minke whales. Be warned, however, that Faraid Head is home to military installations that are in use by the Ministry of Defence, so keep an eye out for red flags or lights, which warn that the headland is off-limits.

The best way to experience the bio-diversity of the headland is to head off on one of the guided walks run by the local countryside ranger. Taking place from June to August, these walks often focus on wildflower identification or puffin spotting; see the Countryside Rangers' website *(p15)* or ask for more details at the Durness Visitor Information Centre.

Top left A puffin perched on the cliffside
Bottom left A pair of guillemots
Right Faraid Head's cliff-lined coastline

NORTHWEST COAST

Start ╎ **Durness**

⋙

End ╎ **Ullapool**

Left Driving past the cloud-topped
Quinag mountain range

NORTHWEST COAST

When people think of the North Coast 500, it's often the raw, elemental beauty of its northwest section that comes to mind. On this stretch, the road heads south from Durness, skirting the edge of remote Cape Wrath – mainland Britain's most northwesterly point – before twisting past hidden beaches, tumbling waterfalls and inky lochs. Before long, the cinematic mountains of Assynt begin to rise on the horizon, as does the rugged Moine Thrust, evidence of a continental collision that took place millions of years ago. These wild landscapes give this section of the route an edge-of-the-world feel, something enhanced by the fact that settlements here are few and far between. But that's not to say you won't find a warm welcome: tiny villages like Scourie and, further south, the bustling fishing settlements of Lochinver and Ullapool provide excellent stopping points for road trippers.

Lewis

Loch
Seaforth

The Minch

Lemreway

N

0 kilometres 5

0 miles 5

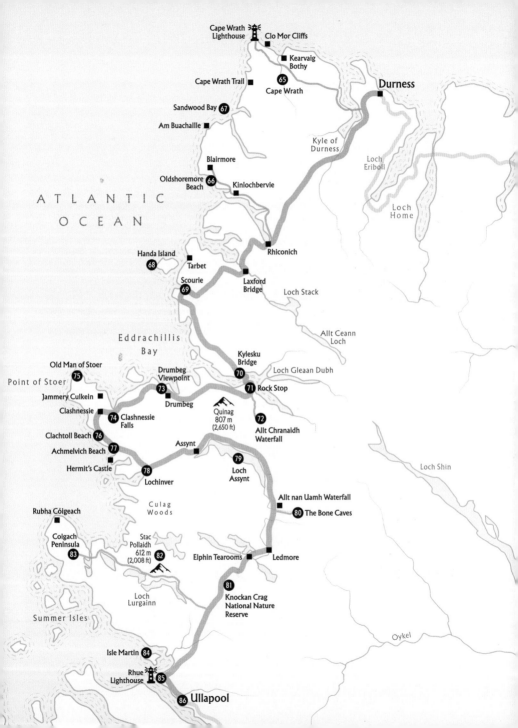

ATLANTIC
OCEAN

Cape Wrath
Lighthouse
Clo Mor Cliffs

Kearvaig
Bothy

Cape Wrath Trail
65 Cape Wrath

Durness

Sandwood Bay **67**

Am Buachaille

Kyle of
Durness

Loch
Eriboll

Blairmore

Oldshoremore **66**
Beach
Kinlochbervie

Loch
Home

Rhiconich

Handa Island
68
Tarbet

Scourie
69

Laxford
Bridge

Loch Stack

*Eddrachillis
Bay*

Allt Ceann
Loch

Kylesku
Bridge
70
Loch Gleann Dubh

Old Man of Stoer
75
Point of Stoer

Drumbeg
Viewpoint
73
Drumbeg

71 Rock Stop

Jammery Culkein

Clashnessie
74 Clashnessie
Falls

Quinag
807 m
(2,650 ft)

72
Allt Chranaidh
Waterfall

Clachtoll Beach **76**

Achmelvich Beach
77

Assynt

Loch Shin

Hermit's Castle

78
Lochinver

79
Loch
Assynt

*Culag
Woods*

Allt nan Uamh Waterfall
80 The Bone Caves

Rubha Cóigeach

Coigach
Peninsula
83

Stac
Pollaidh
612 m
(2,008 ft)
82

Elphin Tearooms
Ledmore

81
Knockan Crag
National Nature
Reserve

Loch
Lurgainn

Summer Isles

Oykel

Isle Martin **84**

Rhue
Lighthouse **85**

86 **Ullapool**

Clockwise from top Getting ready to board the ferry; the lighthouse surrounded by fog; views over Cape Wrath's cliffs

65 Cape Wrath

There's an edge-of-the-world feel to Cape Wrath, mainland Britain's most north-westerly point. It's unsurprising, really, when you consider that this expansive, cliff-lined headland – found well off the route, west of Durness *(p116)* – is actually closer to Iceland than it is to London.

Stretching west from the sand-swept waters of the Kyle of Durness, the cape is made up of mile upon mile of remote moorland, known as the Parph. There was once a community of around 100 people living here, many of them shepherds; today, however, you're more likely to spot a snipe or a meadow pipit than a person. The moorland eventually ends at the cape's dramatic cliffs, which plunge vertically into the foaming waters of the Atlantic. In fact, this spot is home to the Clo Mor Cliffs, the highest sea cliffs on the British mainland, with a sheer drop of 281 m (921 ft). Views stretch across to Orkney and the Outer Hebrides on clear days, but don't count on good weather – sometimes the mist is so thick it's difficult to see more than 100 m (328 ft), but that just makes it all the more atmospheric.

Due to its remoteness, there are only a handful of ways to visit Cape Wrath. Those after an adventure can walk to the cape from Blairmore (northwest of Oldshoremore Beach, *p128*) along the Cape Wrath Trail, a route that weaves all the way from Fort William to the cape. It's only for experienced hikers with navigational skills, though, as much of the route is pathless and requires you to carry your own equipment and supplies (see the WalkHighlands website for more information, *p15*).

For a more easygoing day out, book onto a tour with **Visit Cape Wrath**. This involves a short journey across the Kyle of Durness – usually courtesy of ferryman Malcolm Morrison and his boat *Beulah* – followed by a there-and-back minibus trip to the cape's lighthouse. Expect it to be slow-going: due to the bumpy U70 road, the minibus takes a full hour to make the 18-km (11-mile) trip. Driver Stuart Ross – partial to a dad joke – often quips that the "U" in the road's name stands for useless.

The tour is the most straightforward way to see the cape, but it does lighten the wallet somewhat, with separate charges for the ferry and minibus. To save some pennies, take the ferry across the Kyle and then walk the 18 km (11 miles) along the road to the lighthouse. Not only will you get to take in the moodiness of the moor on foot, there's also the option to overnight in the whitewashed **Kearvaig Bothy** overlooking a stunning golden-sand bay. Two things to bear in mind: there's an MOD range here, so check the firing times on the UK government website (red flags and lights will also provide warning on the ground), and book ahead if you want to hitch a ride back on the minibus from Cape Wrath.

Visit Cape Wrath
W visitcapewrath.com

Kearvaig Bothy
///dust.since.arranger W mountainbothies.org.uk

Roughly 4 km (2 miles) southeast of Oldshoremore Beach, **The Quay House** in Kinlochbervie (///*corrosive.blurred.holly; 01971 521734*) is a great place to refuel. Sat close by the harbour, as its name suggests, this cafe-restaurant serves up heaped helpings of homemade food, including local seafood (the haddock and chips is always a good shout). The cakes are delicious, too.

66 Oldshoremore Beach

///vague.tram.instilled ⬆ 4 km (2.5 miles) northwest of Kinlochbervie on the single-track B801 🅿 Signposted off the B801

From Durness *(p116)*, the road begins to turn south, passing through yet more moody moorland before reaching the tiny hamlet of Rhiconich. From here, it's a 10-km (6-mile) detour northwest along the B801 to reach Oldshoremore Beach, but the extra driving time is more than worth it. This curved bay is dusted with powdery white sand – made from a mix of seashells and limestone – that's dotted by rocky outcrops and fronted by startlingly blue waters. It looks particularly beautiful at sunset, when the light changes its colour to rose gold.

From Oldshoremore, a circular walk north takes in another two stunning beaches: the pale golden sands of Polin and the slightly rockier – but equally beautiful – sweep of Sheigra. The land between them is home to one of mainland Scotland's best examples of machair, a rare, wildflower-rich grassland that supports eight species of orchid and endangered insects like the Great Yellow bumblebee.

67 Sandwood Bay

///slouched.boards.honey 🅿 At Blairmore, 5 km (3 miles) northwest of Kinlochbervie on the single-track B801, followed by a 6.5-km (4-mile) walk 🅦 johnmuirtrust.org

Good-looking beaches might be ten-a-penny in these parts, but if one were to claim the title of most beautiful, it'd be Sandwood Bay. Watched over by grassy dunes and a freshwater loch, this 2.5-km (1.5-mile) sweep of soft pink sand stretches sublimely from high cliffs in the south to rocky moorland in the north. Lapping at its shore is the Atlantic Ocean, on sunny days tinged a surprising turquoise hue. The cherry on top? That'll be Am Buachaille (Gaelic for "the shepherd"), a dramatic finger-like sea stack that rises out of the ocean to the south.

It all sounds rather dreamy, but there's a price to pay for such beauty, and it comes in the form of a 6.5-km (4-mile) walk to reach the bay. That said, it's a pretty easygoing route that winds across peat moorland and around several lochs, apart from the final steep descent down the sand dunes to reach the beach.

For those wanting to keep the beach looking its best, join one of the beach cleans run by the John Muir Trust, which cares for the area; check out the events page on its website for information.

⑥⑧ Handa Island

///most.lashed.cupboards 🏠 5 km (3 miles) off the
A894, signposted to both Tarbet and Handa Island
🅿 On-site at ferry 🕐 Hours vary, check ferry website
Ⓦ Nature reserve: scottishwildlifetrust.org.uk;
Ferry: handa-ferry.com ⛴

A pebble-shaped island within touching
distance of Scotland's west coast, Handa
is one of the most important seabird
breeding colonies in Europe. The cliffs
on the island's northern and western sides
attract a wide variety of species from
April to July every year, including puffins,
razorbills, great skuas and – incredibly –
over 100,000 guillemots.

From April to late August, pedestrian
ferries run from tiny Tarbet on the mainland across to the island, which is cared
for by the Scottish Wildlife Trust. Upon
arrival, a volunteer gives you a short
but engaging introduction to the island,
as well as a map, and then sends you off
to explore. A 6-km (4-mile) loop winds
across the island (keep to the path to
avoid disturbing the birds), taking in
the high cliffs, home to feathered parents
guarding their eggs or hungry chicks
chirping for food, depending on the time
of year. As well as birds, the island also
reveals a whole host of marine mammals,
including otters at Boulders Bay and seals
at Puffin Bay, plus Risso's dolphins, orca
and minke whales out in the Minch (the
stretch of sea between the island and the
Outer Hebrides).

The route also takes in the Great
Stack, a 110-m (361-ft) pillar of Torridon
sandstone, and the remains of an old village
that was abandoned in 1847 following the
potato famine. The latter was once home
to the "Queen of Handa" – a title given to
the oldest widow in the village.

⑥⑨ Scourie

For those interested in fishing, Scourie is
something of a hub, with plenty of salmon
and trout found in the lochs and lochans
surrounding this small village. Fishing
aside, Scourie has a sheltered beach that's
great for sea kayaking, SUPing and
sunset-watching. The village also offers
excellent walking routes nearby, from
headland strolls with views of Handa
Island to hiking adventures up the likes of
Ben Stack, a conical mountain with great
views over the area's rugged landscape.

A keen fisher? Prepared to be reeled in by
Scourie Hotel (///signed.explorer.best;
scouriehotel.com), a family-run spot offering
access to more than 300 fish-filled lochs and
lochans in the area. Even if fishing isn't on
your to-do list, there's plenty to love here,
from the thoughtfully decorated rooms
to the cosy bar warmed by a wood fire.
The restaurant is excellent (if a little
expensive), with a big focus on locally
sourced food, including from the hotel's
own vegetable garden.

⑦ Kylesku Bridge

///cleansed.search.passage
🅿 Northern car park just off the A894
before the bridge; another car park sits after
the southern end of the bridge

As the road curves south from Scourie, the
magnificent glacier-formed mountains of
Scotland's Assynt area come into view, their
rugged forms soaring above the horizon.
It can be a surprise, then, to have this wild
beauty interrupted by the sight of a
concrete bridge – but somehow Kylesku
manages to enhance the scene, perhaps
because its curved form was specifically
designed to blend in with the landscape.

Sweeping across tranquil Loch a' Chàirn
Bhàin, the 276-m- (906-ft-) long bridge
opened in 1984 – before this, the only way
to reach the northern Highlands from here
was via a ferry across the sea loch or by
making a huge detour via Lairg *(p63)*.

For the best views over the bridge (offi-
cially known by its Gaelic name Drochaid
a' Chaolais Chumhaing) and the loch, park
at the car park on its northern side, which
also offers stunning panoramas of Assynt's
mountains. The most distinctive is Quinag,
a horseshoe-shaped trio of peaks popular
with experienced hillwalkers. A ride with
Kylesku Boat Tours provides a different
vantage point: run by Stephen, an experienced skipper, trips takes in the bridge,
nearby lochs and Eas a'Chual Aluinn *(p133)*.
It's a bad day if you don't spot wildlife, too,
whether that's dolphins, seals or sea eagles.

Kylesku Boat Tours
🆆 northwestseatours.co.uk

⑦ Rock Stop

///remark.inert.aspect 🅰 Unapool, Kylesku
🅿 Layby parking on-site 🕒 Apr–Oct:
10am–4pm Sat–Wed 🆆 nwh
geopark.com/exploring/the-rock-stop

This is the visitor centre for the North
West Highlands Geopark, a 2,000-sq-km
(770-sq-mile) area that's home to some of
the oldest rocks in western Europe, as
well as some of the world's earliest fossils.
The free exhibition at the Rock Stop
reveals more of this fascinating geological
history, while its cafe has delicious locally
made cakes and excellent views over the
famed Moine Thrust, which can also be
seen from Knockan Crag *(p144)*.

Above A cyclist crossing the curving arc of Kylesku Bridge

Left Looking down Loch a' Chàirn Bhàin

⓺ Allt Chranaidh Waterfall

///graduated.blotting.readers 🅟 Official car park just off the A894,
near base of waterfall, around 5 km (3 miles) from Kylesku

Allt Chranaidh is for those who like their waterfalls with a touch of drama. Pouring out from the edge of Loch Gainmhich, this 15-m (50-ft) sheet of water cascades down a sheer rock wall before tumbling through a moss-and-lichen-covered gorge. Even its nickname, Wailing Widow Falls, has a story to it. According to legend, a deer hunter once met his end by falling from the top of the falls; the next morning his grief-stricken mother threw herself from the same spot.

The easiest way to see Allt Chranaidh is by parking up in the official car park (a small layby) near its base. From here, it's just a short walk to the bottom of the falls, with epic views up the entire length. Don't wear your finest clothes, though – the path can be rough and muddy.

Another two car parks can be found along the road that winds close to the top of the falls; a gravel one halfway up (with views across Quinag, *p130*) and a rough-and-ready spot near the start of the waterfall. Paths from both lead to the edge of Loch Gainmhich, from where Allt Chranaidh begins its descent. Here, either stick to the south side of the gorge or, for better views, hop across the stream to the northern side. The terrain on each side is incredibly steep and boggy, and there are no guard rails, so it pays to be very cautious. The views of the waterfall from on high, though, are truly stunning.

A visit to Allt Chranaidh can be combined with a longer hike to the top of Eas a' Chual Aluinn. Sliding down a mossy rock face, this ribbon of water is the highest waterfall in Britain, coming in at three times the height of Niagara falls. The walk is a tough one, covering 10 km (6 miles) of first boggy then rough ground, and the near-vertical drop from the top of Eas a' Chual Aluinn is not for the faint hearted. The sight of the falls tumbling into a steep-sided glen and the big-screen beauty of the surrounding Assynt landscape might just make it worth it, though.

Left The impressive form of Allt Chranaidh,
also known as Wailing Widow Falls

🞼 Drumbeg Viewpoint

///billiard.confusion.cucumber 🏠 Signposted just off
the B869 in Drumbeg 🅿 On-site at viewpoint

From Allt Chranaidh, a largely single-track
road twists and turns its way across lonely,
lochan-dotted moorland. It's a beautiful
drive, but a tiring one, making it a relief
to arrive at Drumbeg, a tiny village overlooking a loch to the south and the sea to
the north. There are a handful of places to
shop and stay here, but the real draw is
the Drumbeg Viewpoint, which offers
gorgeous panoramas across the islet-
sprinkled Eddrachillis Bay and surrounding
Assynt coastline. When the weather plays
ball, you can see as far as Handa *(p129)*.

🞽 Clashnessie Falls

///slipped.fussed.sniff 🅿 Opposite the beach, then
2-km (1.5-mile) walk to the falls

Tumbling down a broad rock face lined
by dense bracken, this waterfall gives Allt
Chranaidh *(p132)* a run for its money, especially when in full flow. Even in the drier
summer months, it's a pretty sight, with
twisting strings of water painting the stone.

The falls are reached via a short walk
from Clashnessie village, whose Gaelic
name, Calais an Easaidh, translates as "glen
of the waterfall". While signposted, the
path can be boggy and involves stepping
stones – bring walking boots or wellies.

Before leaving, the village's bay is worth
a look thanks to its pink-tinged sands,
peaceful turquoise waters and mild micro-
climate (it's warmed by the Gulf Stream).

Just off the route in Drumbeg is **Assynt
Aromas** *(////snows.cabbages.generated;
assyntaromas.co.uk)*, a pretty spot run by
mother-and-son team Helen and Danny.
Expect gorgeous candles, soaps and skincare
on sale, all made from natural ingredients by
Helen. Treat yourself to a couple of items
and then head to the shop's on-site Secret
Tea Garden for a mouthwatering slice of cake.

Also in Drumbeg is the aptly named
Drumbeg Stores *(////villas.weeps.opinion;
drumbegstores.co.uk)*, a kind of grocers-cum-
deli with a decent selection of local beers
and whiskies. This one-stop-shop is a great
place to stock up for the road ahead, as well
as browse pieces made by local artisans.

Around 15 km (9 miles) from Drumbeg,
shortly after Clashnessie, a side road leads
to the **Jammery Culkein** *(////tribe.trailing.
bombshell; jammery.co.uk)*. This sweet little
seaside cabin is filled with a selection of jam,
marmalade and chutneys, all made on-site.
But as with many spots along the route,
it's not just a jam shop, also selling
everything from freshly baked bread
to handmade crafts.

🞾 Old Man of Stoer

///plotter.shorthand.support 🏠 Side road off the B869,
1.5 km (1 mile) south of Clashnessie, signposted for
Stoer Head lighthouse 🅿 Stoer Head lighthouse

While less famous than its equally mature
sibling on the Isle of Skye (the Old Man
of Storr), this sliver of a sea stack is just
as striking. Perched off the edge of a

rugged headland northwest of Clashnessie Falls, the Old Man of Stoer rises 60 m (200 ft) out of the ocean, its limestone form regularly whipped by wind and waves. Hardy climbers have been known to tackle the pinnacle – keep an eye out for abseil loops on the summit.

The best way to experience the sea stack is on the 7-km (4.5-mile) loop walk from Stoer Head lighthouse, which traces the top of the cliffs. As well as the Old Man of Stoer, the route takes in some incredible views of the wild coastline and of Assynt's ethereal mountains from the summit of Sìthean Mòr (found behind the sea stack). Whales and dolphins ply the waters here, too, with the Countryside Rangers sometimes hosting wildlife-watching walks *(p15)*.

❼⓺ Clachtoll Beach

///silent.struck.aboard 🏠 Signposted just off the B869 in Clachtoll 🅿 Signposted north of the beach, off a single-track road

Hugged by stony headlands, this pretty pocket of sand stares out across emerald seas towards Lewis and Harris. The water here is so clear that it's a top spot for snorkelling, with the beach one of the stops on the Northwest Highlands Snorkel Trail (run by the **Scottish Wildlife Trust**), alongside the likes of Achmelvich *(p136)* and Gruinard *(p160)*. Everything from urchins to anemones can be spotted, even basking sharks on rare occasions. Above the waves, meanwhile, sea eagles, oystercatchers and skylarks might make an appearance.

Two historical sights lie near the beach. The first is a former salmon bothy, where (if open) you can learn about the area's history from interpretive displays inside; outside sits the remains of poles once used to dry the fishing nets. From here, a short walk along the coast leads to an Iron Age broch (drystone roundtower), known as An Dùn, which is in astonishing condition.

Scottish Wildlife Trust
🅦 scottishwildlifetrust.org.uk

A five-minute walk from Clachtoll Beach is **Flossie's Beach Store** (///pinch.skinning. mavericks; 01571 855222), a great place for a bite to eat whatever the weather. When the sun shines, this bright-blue hut serves up ice creams or chilled soft drink; when there's a chill in the air, it's all about hot chocolates and a comforting hot dog or filled roll. For those campervanning, there's even a wee shop selling the basics (bread, milk, wine).

🖲 Achmelvich Beach

///companies.nerves.carbonate 🏠 Around 10 km
(6 miles) from Clachtoll, signposted off the B869
🅿 Large car park on-site

You would be forgiven for feeling a little beached-out on this stretch, but spare some time for Achmelvich. An arc of white sand bordered by delicate turquoise seas, it actually deserves to be compared to the Caribbean. It's a bit of a ride to get here, with the wiggling single-track road off the B869 giving off rollercoaster vibes. But once you arrive, it's like being in a tropical paradise, with people sunbathing on the sands or taking to the blue waters to SUP or swim (in wetsuits, of course – it's still Scotland, after all).

True, this Blue Flag beach can get a little busy during the summer, but that doesn't detract from its beauty. And for those wanting to explore further, a rough path north across the headland leads to another pristine pocket of sand, which is split into two at high tide. It takes effort to reach though, with eroded sections and some rocky scrambling to contend with.

While it's the sands that may steal your attention, do explore the grassy machair backing them. Come spring and summer, it erupts into colour thanks to an array of wildflowers, among them red clover and mountain thyme, as well as frog, butterfly and heath-spotted orchids. Needless to say, this carpet of petals is great news for pollinators like white-tailed bumblebees, who come to douse themselves in nectar.

On rocky An Farad Bheag headland, just south of the beach, is Hermit's Castle. This miniature concrete fortress was built in the 1950s by an English architect, David Scott, who allegedly fell in love with the beauty of the Highlands. Yet Scott only spent one night in the castle, which took six months to build, before heading back down south and apparently never returning. It still stands today, its angular form blending in surprisingly well with the surrounding headland.

Above Looking over Achmelvich Beach, with its campsite in the background
Right The second beach, north of Achmelvich

● Lochinver

Tucked away at the end of a salty sea loch, this bustling seaside village feels like a metropolis compared to the tiny settlements further north. It's an industrious place, with fishing boats regularly making their way out to sea or coming back laden down with the day's catch. It's also the setting for **Highland Stoneware**, a famed pottery that handcrafts a range of items. Inside, potters fashion the likes of mugs and plates, which are then painted by in-house artists. Outside, old bits of pottery decorate the building's exterior in eye-catching mosaics.

Lochinver makes for a great stop-off point, with some excellent accommodation options, a handful of shops to stock up in and several top-notch cafes. There's plenty to do, too, with walking the biggest draw: a number of excellent strolls can be found a stone's throw away, including a path that threads through nearby community-owned **Culag Wood**. This walk takes in a beautiful pebble beach where otters come to feed, a hilltop viewpoint with stunning mountain vistas, and beautiful forest cloaked in soft green lichen and home to grey heron. »

Pies are the name of the game at the **Lochinver Larder** (///campsites.curtains. heckler; lochinverlarder.com), which has been serving up these filled pastry pots for over 30 years. The menu is extensive, with fillings ranging from venison and cranberry to creamy broccoli, cauliflower and cheese. And for dessert? There are sweet options like apple and cinnamon.

Light, bright and dog-friendly, **Driftwood** (///thankful.remembers.juices) is one of Lochinver's most popular cafes. Alongside top-notch coffee, expect hearty dishes like waffles topped with crispy bacon and delicious home baking, including eye-catching cheesecakes.

As its name suggests, **Inbhir Brunches** (///lordship.cutaway.tweaked; 01571 844746) is the perfect place to fuel up for the day ahead, with filled rolls, avocado toast and more on offer. But where this welcoming spot really shines is with its baked sweet treats: think lemon muffins, berry frangipane and incredibly decadent chocolate cheesecake croissants.

Highland Stoneware
///pushing.awestruck.notch ⌂ Just off Baddidaroch Road 🅿 Large car park on-site ⏰ 9am–5pm Mon–Fri 🌐 highlandstoneware.com/visit-us/lochinver-factory-shop

Culag Wood
///exams.grief.sheep 🅿 Take turning on left after Canisp Road on the A837 in Lochinver, then follow road south past Loch Culag to small signposted car park 🌐 culagwoods.org.uk

Clockwise from top The northern side of Lochinver, seen from the garden area of the Lochinver Larder; snacking on pies from the larder; more views across the sea loch to the village

Another great option for a walk is the loop route (see WalkHighlands, *p15*) that follows the tree-lined River Inver, before cutting across moorland to the beautiful Loch Druim Suardalain, over-looked by Suilven. With its sugar-loaf-shaped hump – known as Caisteal Liath – and rugged ridgeline rising above the moorland, this stunning mountain looks a little otherworldly. You could add a (long) detour to climb it, but it's tough going; despite being only 731 m (2,398 ft) high, the peak has a steep ascent, climb-ing around 500 m (1,640 ft) in only 1 km (0.6 miles).

The village also makes the ideal base from which to set off on adventures to Achmelvich *(p136)*, Quinag *(p130)* and beyond, so it's worth sticking around for a little while, if you have the time.

Instead of taking the main route east upon leaving Lochinver, go south along the single-track road that leads to the Coigach Peninsula *(p146)*. The route is winding, but the loch-and-cnoc landscape is spellbinding (cnoc means "hill" in Gaelic). A couple of viewpoints along the route offer vistas over loch and sea, and there's the option to pull in and walk up to the Falls of Kirkaig. From this waterfall, a track leads all the way to Suilven, whose razor-sharp ridgeline is visible from this vantage point.

Right Loch Druim Suardalain, overlooked by humpbacked Suilven to the right

Above The route curving around Loch Assynt,
with the ruins of Ardvreck Castle on a headland in the background

⑦⑨ Loch Assynt

After Lochinver, the road travels through rocky moorland before skirting the north side of inky Loch Assynt. Look out for paddleboarders, who come to take in the views of the surrounding glacier-crafted mountains; those keen to join them should book in with **Loch, Land and Sea** (which also offers sessions at Achmelvich, *p136*).

If you're more interested in keeping your feet dry, there are several excellent walking trails (see WalkHighlands, *p15*). Near the loch's western end is the wheelchair-friendly Leitir Easaidh Path, which traces a route around two pretty lochs. To the loch's eastern side, meanwhile, a track leads up from tiny Inchnadamph to the Traligill Caves, Scotland's largest cave system. The route winds past three separate caves, but the best is Uamh an Tartair (Cave of the Roaring), where you can see the river gushing below; exploring inside any of the caves is for expert cavers only.

On its northeastern edge, the loch's main highlight is 15th-century Ardvreck Castle, a still-striking ruin sitting on a small promontory. It was constructed in the 15th century by the laird of the Mackenzie clan who, according to legend, received aid from the devil himself to build it. The story goes that the devil asked for the hand of his daughter, Eimhir, in return, but after finding out the identity of her husband, Eimhir threw herself into the loch, transforming into a mermaid. Today, when the water in the loch rises, it's said that she is crying for the life she lost.

Loch, Land and Sea
Ⓦ lochlandandsea.com

⑧⓪ The Bone Caves

///folds.froth.treatment Ⓟ Signposted off the A837, 5 km (3 miles) south of Inchnadamph

There are several reasons why this quartet of caves steals the show. For one thing, they're stunningly situated along the edge of a steep hillside. For another, they're over 200,000 years old. But the most impressive thing about them is the variety of animal bones that have been found inside. First excavated by geologists Peach and Horne in 1889, the caves once contained the remains of everything from birds like widgeon and puffin to apex predators that are now extinct in the UK, such as lynx, brown bears and wolves. Perhaps the most impressive find, though, has to be bone fragments from reindeers, which are thought to be up to 47,000 years old.

Covering just over 2 km (1.5 miles), the walk up to the caves winds through a limestone glen, passing by a pretty waterfall and the Fuaran Allt nan Uamh, a large spring where water can often be seen bubbling up from the ground. Apart from a short, steep section to reach the caves, the path is rather gentle, but those without a head for heights might find the drop down from the caves a bit iffy – although the stunning views back down the glen are enough to make most vertigo-sufferers forget their woes. As for the caves themselves, all four caves can be entered, though exploring any of the openings between them (bar one between the middle two caves) is reserved for experienced cavers.

81 Knockan Crag National Nature Reserve

///amounting.gave.novel 🏠 Signposted off the A835, 18 km (11 miles) from Inchnadamph
🅿 On-site 🕐 24 hrs daily 🌐 nature.scot

From the Bone Caves *(p143)*, the route tracks southwest along the A835, weaving its way through a landscape of craggy hills. As you're driving, a low cliff emerges to the east – it might not seem that special at first glance, but it's actually a globally important geological site. Not only are the rocks at Knockan Crag some of the oldest in the world, but they've also provided scientists with new insights into how our planet was formed. Here, older rocks unusually sit atop younger ones – something that initially baffled 19th-century geologists. Eventually, though, they worked out that this strange phenomenon was caused millions of years ago, when two continents collided and created a "thrust fault" (where the older rocks are pushed to the top of the pile). Knockan Crag is one of the most visible parts of a larger fault – known as the Moine Thrust – that runs from Loch Eriboll *(p110)* on the north coast all the way down to the Isle of Skye in the southwest.

Three interpretive trails explore the area, winding up from an open-air visitor centre containing excellent information boards on the crag's geology and history. The longest walk (1.7 km / 1 mile) is the best, although it can be steep in parts; it traces the edge of the crag to its very top, from where Assynt's cnoc-and-loch landscape unfolds all around. Along the way are poetry excerpts and a number of sculptures, including the *Knockan Puzzle*, a type of geological jigsaw that provides a round-up of Knockan's different rock types.

Those interested in discovering more about the area's geology should visit the Rock Stop *(p130)* near Kylesku. Knockan Crag is also part of the Rock Route, a driving trail that winds from Loch Eriboll to Ullapool and stops at other key geological sights.

Elphin Tearooms *(////opera.compliant.coach; elphintearooms.co.uk)* provide a welcome break on the road between Loch Assynt *(p143)* and Knockan Crag. Housed in an old crofters house, this unassuming spot serves up warming teas and coffees, plus a whole host of tasty treats, including homemade soups, quiches and cakes. There are even locally made arts and crafts items on sale, in case you fancy picking up a souvenir.

Clockwise from top The open-air visitor centre at Knockan Crag; a walker and their dog taking in the view; plants growing around a grey stone

82 Stac Pollaidh

///explored.uniform.skid 🏠 Single-track road off the
A835, 5 km (3 miles) south of Knockan Crag,
signposted for Achiltibuie 🅿 Signposted off
single-track road

One of Assynt's most striking mountains,
Stac Pollaidh and its crinkled ridge looms
above the surrounding boggy green moorland. A 4.5-km (2.8-mile) walking trail
circuits its base, with views north out
towards Suilven *(p140)* and southwest to
the Summer Isles *(p148)*, while Assynt's
eerily beautiful loch-and-cnoc landscape
is on fine display all around.

While Stac Pollaidh is rather short
in stature at only 612 m (2,008 ft) high,
its summit – at the western end – involves
scaling a series of rocky towers and so is
only accessible to experienced mountain-
eers. The slightly lower peak at its eastern
end can be tackled as part of the above
loop walk, although it does require a bit
of scrambling.

Left A cyclist pedalling towards Stac Pollaidh, whose
rugged ridge is seen to the left in the background

❽ Coigach Peninsula

This loch-dotted peninsula sprawls west from Knockan Crag. A bit of a detour off-route, it's accessed via a winding single-track road that passes by a trio of vast lochs and a series of mountains, among them Stac Pollaidh *(p146)* and the hulking form of Ben Mór Coigach.

A big draw is **Achnahaird Beach**, a pocket of creamy sand on the peninsula's northeast coast. The beach expands dramatically at low tide, becoming roughly three times longer than it is wide, while wildlife-filled rock pools appear in the craggy granite surrounding it. The dunes and machair bordering the beach support many species, from plants like mosses and liverworts to birds such as lapwings and sandpipers; even golden eagles sometimes drop by for a visit. The whole scene is watched over by the mountains of Assynt, which rise impressively to the east.

On the peninsula's southern side is Achiltibuie, which can be reached on a narrow single-track road from Achnahaird. Skirting the shore of Loch Broom, this tiny crofting village is home to a handful of shops and the excellent **FISK Gallery**, selling works by local artists. The settlement is also a jumping-off point for access to the Summer Isles, a collection of craggy islands, islets and skerries scattered offshore. Known for its beautiful white-sand beach, Isle Ristol is the closest to the mainland and can be reached on foot at low tide. To visit most of the rest, though, a boat trip with the likes of **Shearwater Cruises** is in order, or perhaps a kayak tour with **Kayak Summer Isles**, which takes in craggy caves and sandy beaches;

there's also the option to wild camp overnight. Whatever you decide, there's a good chance of spotting wildlife, such as seals and dolphins.

Achnahaird Beach
///units.employer.enclosing ⌂ 13 km (8 miles) west of Stac Pollaidh along single-track road
🅿 On-site west of the beach

FISK Gallery
///reds.fence.browsers ⌂ 205 Polbain, Achiltibuie
🅿 On-site ⏱ Hours vary, check website
🌐 fisk-gallery-achiltibuie.co.uk

Shearwater Cruises
🌐 summerqueen.co.uk

Kayak Summer Isles
🌐 kayaksummerisles.com

❽ Isle Martin

///uplifting.washed.flopped ⌂ Ferries from Ardmair Jetty 🅿 Long layby off the A835 in Ardmair, then walk carefully alongside the road to the jetty ⏱ Ferry times vary, check website 🌐 islemartin.org

As the A835 meanders south towards Ullapool, skirting pebbly Ardmair Beach, the humped silhouette of Isle Martin appears on the horizon. It's worth making the short ferry ride from the jetty – found near the beach – to this island in Loch Broom, which is completely traffic free and has been community-owned since 1999.

Despite its rather diminutive size, there's plenty to explore. There's a micro-museum covering the island's history, from its time as a monastic settlement to its role in the

Above Isle Martin, emerging out of the shimmering waters of Loch Broom

herring industry, and a brilliantly named "library of stuff" that contains everything from wetsuits and wellies (for hire) to a small pop-up cafe (its opening hours are irregular). For walkers, a number of rough and sometimes boggy trails lead to the island's summit, where there are views across the sea to the mainland, including imposing Ben Mór Coigach. There's bothy-style and cottage accommodation on the island, too, for those wanting to spend the night, plus the freedom to wild camp. And for those good samaritans out there, volunteering days are occasionally run to help with the upkeep of the island (think path maintenance) – check the website for more details.

85 Rhue Lighthouse

///stickler.executive.peanut ⌂ Single-track road off the A835, 1.6 km (1 mile) south of Ardmair, signposted for Rhue ℗ Signposted off single-track road

This tiny lighthouse might not be much to look at, but the views beyond it are well worth the short walk from the car park. From the lighthouse's craggy location, inky Loch Broom stretches out towards the emerald Summer Isles, while the imposing peaks of Beinn Ghobhlach and Ben Mór Coigach rise to the south and north. The walk in from the car park is pretty picturesque, too, tracing the coastline past a small beach.

⑧⑥ Ullapool

It might hold the title of the northwest's biggest town, but Ullapool is actually relatively compact. Yet what it lacks in size, it more than makes up for with a stunning location – surrounded by mountains on the edge of Loch Broom – and a pleasingly energetic air, thanks in no small part to its industrious fishing harbour. All that's before mentioning the town's abundance of excellent restaurants and cafes, which feed both hardworking locals and hungry travellers, and often host performances of traditional Scottish music. And to top it all off? There's even a Tesco, a rare sight elsewhere on this stretch of coast.

All of this makes Ullapool a place to linger, not least along its pretty harbourside. Here, a row of whitewashed cottages overlooks the mountain-encircled Loch Broom, dotted with fishing boats and pleasure craft. Admittedly the large ferry terminal nearby – which runs daily boats to Stornoway on Lewis – detracts slightly from the scene, but not by much.

For the best views, hike up to the top of Meall Mòr, the 270-m (886-ft) hill just behind the town (see WalkHighlands for more information, *p15*). From its summit, the gridded streets of Ullapool feel like a toytown, and views across Loch Broom, the Summer Isles and the surrounding rugged mountains unfurl before you. Countryside Rangers sometimes offer guided walks up the hill, as well as longer hikes around the area, plus citizen science projects to count butterflies – see the Countryside Rangers website for more details *(p15)*. »

Run by two west coasters, Fenella Renwick and Kirsty Scobie, the **Seafood Shack** (///blinking.calendars.shorten; seafoodshack. co.uk) is a temple to ocean ingredients. Everything is sourced fresh from the surrounding sea on a daily basis, with Kirsty's husband bringing in much of the catch. The huge haddock wrap is an undoubted winner, but don't skip the juicy langoustines or salty oysters either.

Owned by Zoë McClunie, who hails from Christchurch in New Zealand, **Cult Cafe** (///automate.amid.intrigues; 01854 612995) brings a touch of Kiwi cool to Ullapool's shores. Inside, dried flowers hang from the ceiling and expert baristas serve up superb coffees (possibly the best on the whole route) alongside tasty home baking. There are excellent breakfast and brunch options, too.

Clockwise from top left The Seafood Shack, with its outdoor seating area; sampling some oysters from the shack; looking over Ullapool's pretty harbour, dotted with boats

Above An artist painting a mug in Ullapool's Highland Stoneware pottery
Above right Finished items painted with Highland scenes on display

The friendly staff are more than happy to chat, or you can simply watch them at work before browsing the beautifully finished products.

Ullapool Museum
///swanky.furniture.pots ⬛7 & 8 West Argyle Street 🅿 Latheron Lane car park 🕐 11am–4pm Mon–Sat, noon–4pm Sun 🅦 ullapoolmuseum.co.uk 🔗

Highland Stoneware
///slurping.announce.narrowest ⬛ Signposted off the A835, where North Road and Mill Street meet 🅿 On-site 🕐 9am–5pm Mon–Sat 🅦 highland stoneware.com/visit-us/ullapool-factory-shop

In the town itself is the **Ullapool Museum**, housed in a 19th-century parish church designed by Scottish civil engineer Thomas Telford. Largely run by volunteers, this humble yet interesting spot is all about local history; exhibits touch on topics such as crofting and fishing, as well as emigration – in 1773, many crofters left Scotland from this spot, sailing off for new lives in Canada's Nova Scotia.

On the edge of town, just off the North Coast 500, there's the second branch of the Highland Stoneware pottery. As with the Lochinver site *(p139)*, a small team of craftspeople produce stunning items of pottery: throwing the clay, firing it in a kiln and then decorating it, whether that's by hand-painting or glazing using locally sourced stones.

A pretty whitewashed building in the heart of Ullapool, the **Ceilidh Place** (///clubs. lived.query; theceilidhplace.com) offers simple yet comfortable rooms; thoughtful touches include the small "libraries" in each room, with books curated by locals. And in true Highlands style, this isn't just a hotel: it's also home to a cute bookshop and a cafe-restaurant where live music is played.

Overlooking Loch Broom, just 5 km (3 miles) southeast of Ullapool, is **Ecotone Cabins** (///skim.brushing.airports; ecotonecabins.com). These two wooden cabins are wonderfully eco-friendly, being made from sustainable materials and powered by renewable energy. And that's not the only way the Planterose family, who own the cabins, are helping the natural environment. Among other projects, they're rewilding the surrounding woodland and have set up an on-site organic croft.

WEST COAST

Start **Ullapool**

End **Inverness**

Left The sands of Gruinard Beach,
surrounded by rugged hills

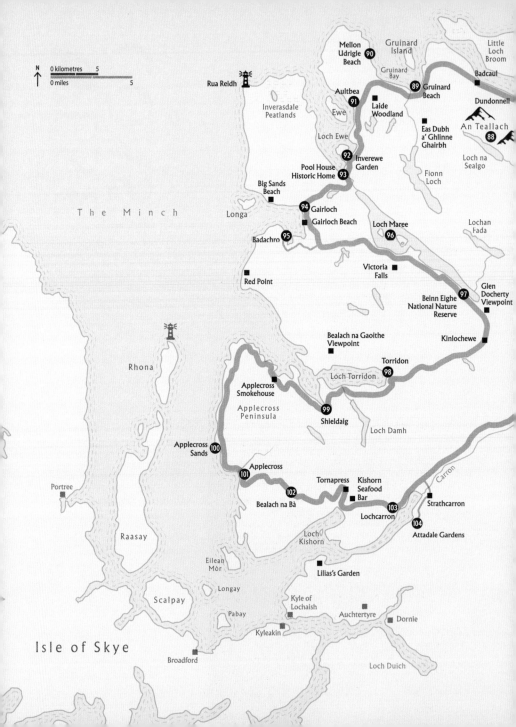

N
0 kilometres 5
0 miles 5

Rua Reidh

Inverasdale
Peatlands

The Minch

Gruinard
Island

Mellon
Udrigle
Beach **90**

Gruinard
Bay

Little
Loch
Broom

Badcaul

89 Gruinard
Beach

Dundonnell

An Teallach
88

Aultbea
91

Laide
Woodland

Eas Dubh
a' Ghlinne
Ghairbh

Loch na
Sealgo

Ewe

Loch Ewe

92 Inverewe
Garden

Pool House
Historic Home **93**

Fionn
Loch

Big Sands
Beach

Longa

94 Gairloch

Gairloch Beach

Loch Maree

Lochan
Fada

Badachro **95**

Loch Maree **96**

Red Point

Victoria
Falls

Beinn Eighe
National Nature
Reserve

97

Glen
Docherty
Viewpoint

Rhona

Bealach na Gaoithe
Viewpoint

Kinlochewe

Torridon

98

Loch Torridon

Applecross
Smokehouse

Applecross
Peninsula

99
Shieldaig

Loch Damh

Applecross
Sands **100**

101 Applecross

Portree

102

Tornapress

Kishorn
Seafood
Bar

Carron

Strathcarron

Raasay

Bealach na Bà

103
Lochcarron

104
Attadale Gardens

Eilean
Mòr

Longay

Loch
Kishorn

Lilias's Garden

Scalpay

Pabay

Kyle of
Lochaish

Auchtertyre

Dornie

Kyleakin

Broadford

Isle of Skye

Loch Duich

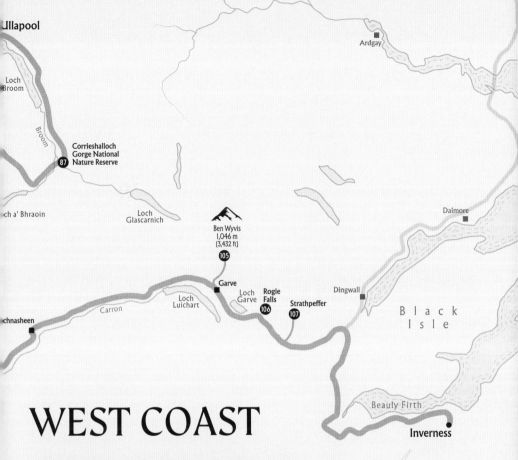

WEST COAST

Upon leaving Ullapool, the route keeps largely close to the coast, tracing a line around the edge of several twinkling sea lochs lined by pretty villages and sandy bays. As with the northwest section, the landscapes here have a feeling of wild beauty to them: Torridon's hulking mountains and the impressive gorge at Corrieshalloch are just two standouts. Stretches of the road can feel pretty untamed, too, with exciting single-track sections found between Dundonnel and Gairloch and around the edge of the Applecross Peninsula. The crowning glory of the road itself has to be the Bealach na Bà, a soaring mountain pass that zigzags down towards the whitewashed houses of Lochcarron. From here, the route sets course east once more, flattening out as it makes its way back to Inverness – the welcoming end of the North Coast 500.

❽ Corrieshalloch Gorge National Nature Reserve

///aimed.asking.puddles ⌂ Braemore Junction, Loch Broom, Garve
🅿 Large car park on-site 🕐 Gorge: 24 hrs daily; visitor centre and cafe:
May–Nov: 9.30am–4pm daily Ⓦ nts.org.uk

From Ullapool *(p150)*, the North Coast 500 stretches alongside Loch Broom, before following the course of its namesake river inland to Corrieshalloch. This spot's Gaelic name translates as "ugly hollow", but this couldn't be further from the truth: this gorge is stunningly beautiful. Covered with mosses and ferns, the ravine's steep-sided walls plunge vertiginously downwards for 60 m (200 ft), enclosing a ribbon-like waterfall known as the Falls of Measach. This masterpiece of nature has taken a while to create: it was formed over millions of years by glacial meltwater, which flowed down from nearby Loch Broom.

From the car park near the excellent visitor centre – which comes complete with a welcoming takeaway cafe, toilets and EV charging points – a path leads down through shady woodland. While the main event is undoubtedly the gorge itself, the woodland walk here is a peaceful experience, with a further two gushing waterfalls to be admired. Eventually, the 150-year-old suspension bridge that crosses the gorge comes into view. Commissioned by Sir John Fowler – creator of both the London Underground and Edinburgh's Forth Bridge – this impressive construction was the UK's first cable suspension bridge (cable replaced chains). Crossing the bridge provides a spectacular bird's-eye view of the gorge and the Falls of Measach, although even those without vertigo might feel a little dizzy looking down. Beyond, the path winds around to another viewing platform that juts out over the gorge and offers even more amazing vistas.

It might be hard to gaze away from the gorge, but there's plenty of flora and fauna to spot here, too – after all, Corrieshalloch is also a nature reserve. Trees like pine, oak and hazel flank the sides of the gorge, while a whole array of moisture-loving ferns sprout from its walls and in the surrounding woodland. Lady Fowler's fern walk – named after Sir John's wife – is a great place to spy the latter. For keen wildlife watchers, Corrieshalloch also offers the chance to see golden eagles wheeling in the skies above and red squirrels nibbling on pine cones. For more information on the area's environmental importance, chat to one of the friendly on-site rangers at the visitor centre.

Right Corrieshalloch gorge and waterfall, crossed by
the suspension bridge, seen from the viewing platform

🔵88 An Teallach

///blackouts.vocals.listening 🏠 22 km (14 miles) northwest of Corrieshalloch 🅿 Large layby off the A832,
roughly 250 m (820 ft) east of Dundonnell Hotel

The west coast is known for its impressive
mountains, including the likes of Slioch
and Stac Pollaidh *(p146)*. Joining their
ranks is An Teallach, a brawny mountain
range with two Munros: Sgurr Fiona and
Bidein a'Ghlas Thuill. Climbing the
mountain, which is reached from the
tiny hamlet of Dundonnell, is best left
to experienced hillwalkers, as it involves
traversing a rocky, narrow ridge. But
for those with the skills to try it, it's one
of the best mountain climbs in the UK,
with stunning views across the surrounding
mountainous landscape. See WalkHighlands
(p15) for more information.

🔵89 Gruinard Beach

///bound.relations.residual 🏠 20 km (12 miles)
west of Dundonnell 🅿 Signposted off the A832

Several beautiful beaches dot the shoreline
of expansive Gruinard Bay, but Gruinard
Beach itself has to be a highlight. Encircled
by craggy green hills, this pink-gold beach
takes its hue from the area's Torridonian
Sandstone, a colour that contrasts rather
dramatically with the bay's emerald sea.

A short boardwalk leads down from
the car park to the sands, which look out
towards velvety green Gruinard Island,
most famous as the site of biological
warfare experiments in World War II.
There are plenty of wildlife-filled

rockpools dotted here and there on the
beach, each one containing its own miniature ocean ecosystem, with everything
from shrimps to sea squirts on show.

The beach is a great spot to get out
and stretch your legs. If you're wanting
to explore a little further, take the short –
if muddy – walk that leads inland along
the river, ending at the pretty Eas Dubh
a' Ghlinne Ghairbh waterfall.

Top tip: the road just south of here
winds uphill to a layby. Make sure to stop
and get out – the views back towards the
beach are incredible.

A cute log cabin, **Rocklea** (////reviews.quirky.
incurring; rocklea-lg.com) has a lot going for
it. The first is its location, just a short walk
from the sweeping sands of Gruinard Beach.
The second is the views, which take in both
the beach and the wider bay, including out
to Gruinard Island. And the third? It's
literally a hop, skip and a jump off the route.

Roughly 6 km (4 miles) west of Gruinard
Beach is **Gruinard Bay Caravan Park**
(gruinardbay.co.uk; ///buyers.unzipped.
parrot). Overlooking a shingly beach, this
is another spot with beautiful views out
across the bay – you might even spot eider
ducks, otters and dolphins in the water.
There are touring pitches for caravans,
motorhomes and tents, as well as five
holiday caravans for hire.

90 Mellon Udrigle Beach

///loitering.conveys.translate ⌂ 11 km (7 miles) northwest of Gruinard Beach; signposted turning for Mellon Udrigle P Off single-track road to northwest of beach

If any beach in the area could give Gruinard a run for its money, it's Mellon Udrigle. Found 5 km (3 miles) off the North Coast 500, this dusky white beach is made from fine shell sand, making it a soft delight to walk on, and is fringed by clear seas that shine turquoise on sunny days.

The beach is beautiful, but the views of the mountains are the main highlight. To the north, look out for Suilven's distinctive outline *(p140)*, the mountains of Coigach *(p148)* and the saw-toothed ridge of Stac Pollaidh *(p146)*; to the south-east sits the folded peaks of An Teallach. More rocky delights can be found close by, with stony promontories bookending the beach. At low tide they reveal rockpools, filled with the likes of starfish and crabs.

In the dunes behind the beach is an Iron Age hut circle made from red sandstone, as well as a couple of shell middens. Heading northwest from the beach, a rough path makes a loop around a windswept headland; the views over Gruinard Bay, the Summer Isles and the mountains of Coigach and Assynt are spectacular. A couple of other excellent walks can be found in **Laide Woodland**, a community-owned spot home to white-tailed eagles, otters and a beautiful waterfall.

Laide Woodland
W laidewood.org.uk

91 Aultbea

Blink-and-you'll-miss-it Aultbea is a tiny fishing village overlooking Loch Ewe, just off the North Coast 500. It's definitely worth a stop, not least to visit the **Arctic Convoy Museum**. This volunteer-run spot recounts the story of the British convoys who set off from Loch Ewe during World War II, braving icy conditions and the wrath of German U-boats to deliver much-needed supplies to Russia after it was attacked by the Nazis. The displays – which include model ships, weapons and photographs – are a little homely in feel, but they serve their purpose well.

Aultbea's other draw is the excellent **Ewe Canoe**, run by experienced guide Conor, who offers kayaking and canoeing trips of the area's sea and inland lochs, including Loch Ewe itself. Expect rugged coastline, rocky channels and a fair bit of wildlife watching, with otters, seals and porpoise all calling the area home.

Arctic Convoy Museum
///boils.observer.fattest ⌂ Birchburn; signposted off the A832 P On-site ⏱ 10am–4pm Mon–Sat W racmp.co.uk ⚡

Ewe Canoe
W ewecanoe.co.uk

⑨² Inverewe Garden

///even.rift.suspended 🏠 Poolewe; signposted
off the A832 🅿 Large car park on-site 🕐 10am–5pm
daily (Nov–Apr: to 3pm) 🌐 nts.org.uk 🔀

From Aultbea *(p161)*, the North Coast
500 wriggles its way alongside Loch Ewe.
At the southern end of this huge sea
loch, a surprising sight emerges from
the otherwise rugged coastline: a lush
and colourful garden. This is Inverewe,
a botanical treasure trove created in the
late 19th century by Osgood Mackenzie.

Alongside native plants, Mackenzie
sowed species from around the world,
including electric-blue Himalayan poppies,
towering Californian redwoods and
mottled Tasmanian eucalyptus, as well as
more rhododendrons than you can shake a
stick at. Some of those he planted were
subtropical species, which thrived despite
the garden's wild location, thanks to the
warming effects of the Gulf Stream.
After Mackenzie's death, his legacy was
carried on by his daughter, Mairi, who
built Inverewe House among the foliage;
it's now home to an interactive museum
that delves into the history of the gardens.

Today, Inverewe covers a staggering
22 hectares (55 acres), making it easy
to find a peaceful pocket to yourself even
in the height of summer. A network of
paths laces through the gardens, of which
there are more than a dozen, each thriving
under the eye of expert on-site gardeners.
An undoubted highlight is the oceanside »

Right The Walled Garden at Inverewe, bordering
the sea and filled with fruit and vegetables

Above Steps leading down into the Walled Garden

Top right A bee visiting some thistle-like sea holly

Bottom right Martin Hughes, operations manager at Inverewe, admiring some gunnera

Walled Garden (the first to be built here), bursting with fruit trees and vegetables, all grown organically. Other leafy must-sees include the Savage Garden, which seethes with carnivorous plants, and the Forest Garden, home to a number of Mackenzie's famed rhododendrons, some of which are more than 120 years old.

The waters around the garden can be explored, too, with local skipper and scallop diver Jamie Elder offering regular boat trips via **West Highland Marine Ltd**. Expect to see wildlife both above and below the water, from sea eagles and herons to lobsters, starfish and crabs (the latter hauled up by fishing creels and pots).

Back in the garden, however, it's not all a bed of roses. Inverewe is beginning to see the negative effects of climate change, particularly ferocious storms that can cause damage. But the gardeners here are fighting back. A nursery has been set up to grow new saplings from the pine cones of trees felled by recent storms, which will eventually be planted out on the old site of the parent tree. There's a pollinator planting scheme, too, and a canny reuse of biodegradable packaging from the on-site cafe; over 30 tonnes of compost is made annually and returned (along with a nutrient-rich biochar) to the earth's soil. According to the folks at Inverewe, it's all about making things as circular as possible, so that the garden can continue to flourish well into the future.

West Highland Marine Ltd
W westhighlandmarine.co.uk

❿ Pool House Historic Home

///loops.canal.copiers Poolewe; signposted off the A832 🅿 On-site ⏲ Hours vary, check website 🅦 pool-house.co.uk 🔁 📷

Once home to the Mackenzie clan, this 300-year-old manor house is beautifully located on the edge of Loch Ewe, just south of Inverewe Garden. Admirable setting aside, it's the art and antiques inside that draw the crowds: cute-as-a-button doll's houses, beautifully painted bone china, scale models of ships and trains, it's all here. Entry is by guided tour, which recalls Pool House's long-standing history, including its time as an 18th-century courthouse and World War II headquarters; it was even home to Inverewe Garden's Osgood Mackenzie (p162) for a while in the 19th century. On some Thursdays, tours can take a spooky turn – because any old manor house worth its salt must be home to a poltergeist or two.

❾ Gairloch

Looking out over its namesake loch and the Torridon mountains, Gairloch is a collection of pretty cottages and crofters' houses strung along a beach-peppered coastline. This down-to-earth town is pretty small (despite being the second-largest town on the west coast after Ullapool), but it still has plenty going for it. For one thing, there's the **Gairloch Museum**, an award-winning spot telling

The cafe in Gairloch's welcoming **GALE Centre** (////poorly.investors.moves; galeactionforum.co.uk) serves up everything from healthy salads to delicious cakes baked by locals. There's also a handy tourist information service and an on-site shop, packed with items made by local crafters. The best thing, though? All of the centre's profits go back into community projects. If you want to do your bit to help, use the centre's "pay it forward" scheme. Here, you can pay for an additional meal, so that locals – especially those who might be struggling to make ends meet – can have free or discounted meals during winter.

the history of the area. Inside, highlights include carved Pictish stones, a 19th-century outdoor pulpit and a monumental Fresnel lens that once sat in nearby Rua Reidh Lighthouse. Outside, behind the museum, the 3-km (2-mile) Achtercairn archaeology trail winds past 12 well-preserved Iron Age roundhouses.

The excellent museum aside, the town really excels in outdoor activities, whether that's walks in Flowerdale Glen or wildlife-watching boat trips (operators **Hebridean Whale Cruises** and **Gairloch Marine Life Centre & Cruises** both offer tours).

And if it's beaches you're looking for, Gairloch has them in spades. To the south is **Gairloch Beach**, a rose-gold stretch of sand surrounded by dunes; after these grassy hillocks were damaged by a storm in the early 1990s, determined locals moved 5,000 tonnes of sand to help repair

Above The GALE Centre in Gairloch,
home to a cafe, shop and visitor information centre

them. North, meanwhile, is the aptly
named **Big Sands Beach**, a quieter swathe
of shingley sand offering, on a clear day,
views out to the distant Hebrides.

A little further on from Big Sands,
perched on the edge of a moor-blanketed
headland, is Rua Reidh Lighthouse. While
the building and its grounds are now
private accommodation (and so are off-
limits), you can wander east from here,
along rough and narrow cliff paths, and
past dramatic sea stacks, to reach Camas
Mor, a beautiful beach surrounded by
bright green cliffs. Take the steep sheep
track down to the beach or make a loop
back to the lighthouse (see WalkHighlands
for more information, *p15*).

Gairloch Museum
///album.await.auctioned 🅿 Signposted off
the A832 🕒 Apr–Oct: 10am–5pm Mon–Sat
Ⓦ gairlochmuseum.org

Hebridean Whale Cruises
Ⓦ hebridean-whale-cruises.co.uk

Gairloch Marine Life Centre & Cruises
Ⓦ porpoise-gairloch.co.uk

Gairloch Beach
///difficult.repay.inhales 🅿 Signposted off the A832

Big Sands Beach
///propelled.unicorns.condition 🏠 6 km (4 miles) from
Gairloch, signposted off the A832 🅿 North of the beach

95 Badachro

Don't let Badachro fool you. This tiny fishing village – no more than a smattering of houses overlooking a curving bay – has a lot going on.

The first port of call has to be the excellent **Badachro Distillery**, run by Gordon and Vanessa Quinn. The pair first met 40 years ago at Badachro's local inn and, after living in places as far afield as Saudi Arabia, returned to the west coast to raise their family. Inspired by a love of gin and the area's wealth of botanicals, including wild bog myrtle, seaweed and wild thyme, they experimented with different gins – and so Badachro Distillery was born. Today, this small indie spot produces award-winning gin, vodka and, of course, whisky, with intimate tours taking you through the distilling process and ending with a tasting session in the sun room of Gordon and Vanessa's house (it's right next door).

Near the distillery, a stepped path leads down to the coast, where a pontoon stretches across to Dry Island. This rocky islet is home to born-and-bred fisherman Ian McWhinney, who's been fishing these waters for shellfish for over 40 years. As well as bringing in the daily catch, Ian also runs (alongside his trusty dog Dubh) the fantastic **Shellfish Safari** tours, which are focused on sustainable fishing, a topic close to his heart. The 90-minute tours involve an entertaining yet educational trip out to sea on Ian's boat, the *Iona*, to reel in a creel and see what's been caught. Regular finds include velvet swimming crabs, langoustines and – unique to Scotland's west coast – squat lobsters. Back on dry land, Ian uses the day's catch to cook up a tasty lunch. Food doesn't come fresher than this. »

Badachro Distillery
///scratches.sunset.lectures ⌂ Aird Hill, 11 km (7 miles) from Gairloch; signposted to Badachro off the A832 🅿 On-site 🕓 Tours: hours vary, check website; shop: 10am–4pm Mon–Fri Ⓦ badachrodistillery.com 🔗 For tours 🔗

Shellfish Safari
///smirking.cheesy.reason ⌂ Dry Island, 11 km (7 miles) from Gairloch; signposted to Badachro off the A832 🅿 Small parking bay above Dry Island, 0.3 km (0.2 miles) northeast of Badachro Distillery, followed by short walk 🕓 Tours: hours vary, check website Ⓦ shellfishsafari.co.uk 🔗 🔗

Right on the edge of the harbour, **Badachro Inn** (////crowns.toasted.laces; badachroinn.com) is the perfect spot for an evening drink. Tipples on offer include everything from local ales to malt whiskies, plus spirits made by the village's own Badachro Distillery (Vanessa and Gordon are regulars here). Hunker down in the snug bar area or pull up a chair in the conservatory, whose big windows take in views of the bay beyond.

Clockwise from top left A pile of creels used for fishing; Dubh the dog;
a plate of shellfish; Ian, the owner of Shellfish Safaris

Beyond Badachro, a single-track road winds coast-side to remote Red Point, a mere wisp of a hamlet. The headland just beyond here, covered in springy heather, is the setting for two beautiful **beaches** – fittingly named North Beach and South Beach – both famed for their striking crimson-coloured sand. North Beach is the more accessible of the two, although it still requires a bit of a jaunt from the car park through steep-sided sand dunes to reach it. It's a great spot for a dip, too, with stunning views out towards the isles of Skye, Lewis and Harris. South Beach requires a longer walk along farm tracks, but is even more secluded, with dramatic panoramas towards the Applecross Peninsula. A 5-km (3-mile) circular walk loops around the headland to connect the two beaches, doubling down on the incredible views as it goes – keep your eyes peeled for porpoises, otters and seabirds along the way.

Red Point Beaches
///hindering.decisions.conclude 🅿 10 km (6 miles) southwest of Badachro along single-track road, followed by a roughly 200-m (650-ft) walk to North Beach and a 1-km (0.6-mile) walk to South Beach

Right Looking across the red sands of North Beach

96 Loch Maree

As the A832 slinks southeast, it skirts the edge of this impressive loch. Scotland's fourth-largest body of water, Loch Maree stretches around 20 km (13 miles) in length and is lined dramatically by mountains on either side (Slioch is a fine challenge for experienced hikers).

On the loch's metallic-grey waters are over 40 jigsaw-shaped islands, most of them blanketed by ancient pines – a remnant of the original Caledonian forest that once covered much of Scotland. They're home to a variety of rare birds and insects, with the islands an important breeding ground for the likes of black-throated divers. The loch's biggest island, Eilean Sùbhainn, is a little unusual for having its own loch, within which lies another island. This makes the latter, wonderfully, rather like a Russian doll: it's an island within a loch on an island within a loch. To get out on the water, take a tour with **Gairloch Kayak Centre**, which offers full-day adventures.

There are a couple of other spots around the loch that are worth a stop, including the tumbling **Victoria Falls** – reached via a short, accessible path from a nearby car park – and little Kinlochewe, a small settlement with a smattering of great places to eat. For those looking for a quintessential Highland scene, **Glen**

Docherty Viewpoint, at the southeastern end of the loch, is a must-visit. Here, the A832 zigzags through a heather-and-bracken-painted glen towards the mountain-encircled Loch Maree, which stretches effortlessly into the distance.

Gairloch Kayak Centre
W gairlochkayakcentre.com

Victoria Falls
///pool.intelligible.incur P 15 km (9 miles) from Gairloch; signposted off the A832 W forestryandland.gov.scot

Glen Docherty Viewpoint
///elects.enchanted.issues P 5 km (3 miles) southeast of Kinlochewe; signposted off the A832

Around 3 km (2 miles) from the southeastern end of the loch, **Kinlochewe Hotel** (///parked.honestly.corner; kinlochewe hotel.co.uk) started life as a coaching inn in the 19th century, providing rest to weary coachmen and their horses. Today, this whitewashed stone building remains a warm and welcoming place, with comfortable rooms and hearty local food, the latter courtesy of The Stag restaurant on-site.

Clockwise from top Gazing down to Loch Maree from Glen Docherty Viewpoint; a red deer roaming the surrounding hills; a kayaker out on the loch

⑰ Beinn Eighe National Nature Reserve

Stretching southwest of Loch Maree, this national nature reserve was the first to be established in the UK, in 1951. It's named after the soaring mountain at its heart, the 1,010-m (3,310-ft) Beinn Eighe, one of three main peaks in the Torridon area (the other two are Beinn Alligin and Liathach, *p176*). Made from Torridonian Sandstone, the mountains here are astoundingly old, dating back almost 750 million years. Yet despite their age, they are bursting with life. A whole host of plants live here, including rare mosses and ancient pinewoods (some of the more senior "granny pines" are over 350 years old). These in turn provide habitat for birds like golden eagles and mammals like wildcats and red deer.

The best place to start exploring is at the **Visitor Centre**. Inside are engaging displays on the reserve's geology, geography and wildlife, including a helpful 3D map to get you oriented; friendly staff are also on-hand to provide advice on different walks in the area. Several trails of varying difficulties start from here, with two more beginning at the Coille na Glas-Leitir car park, just 2.5 km (1.5 miles) northwest. For those looking to climb Beinn Eighe itself, head down Glen Torridon, a valley to the southwest of Kinlochewe, from where a loop walk begins and ends (see WalkHighlands for more details, *p15*).

Visitor Centre
///atlas.crazy.chilling 🅿 1.6 km (1 mile) northwest of Kinlochewe; signposted off the A832 🕐 Apr–Oct: 10am–5pm daily 🆆 nature.scot

Above The road through Glen Torridon,
from where the walk up Beinn Eighe begins

98 Torridon

At the end of Glen Torridon, the road passes through tiny Torridon village. Although little more than a sparse group of houses, this village still makes an impression thanks to its spectacular location on the edge of a loch, with the Torridon mountains rising like stone sentries behind. Needless to say, the village is a great place for walkers to base themselves, with unparalleled hiking available in the surrounding area, much of which is cared for by the National Trust for Scotland (NTS). As well as Beinn Eighe, there's the option to climb towering Beinn Alligin, famous for its rocky "horns", and Liathach, a ridge-backed mountain with two peaks, although both routes are extremely challenging. The village's Countryside Centre once had information on the area's hiking routes, but at the time of writing it was closed for development – check out the WalkHighlands website *(p15)* instead.

Torridon's sea loch is also ideal for salty adventures. Based in The Torridon, a five-star hotel, **Torridon Outdoors** runs kayaking trips, with near-guaranteed chances of spotting local wildlife like otters and sea eagles. Meanwhile, the Torridon Snorkel Trail – run by the Scottish Wildlife Trust – takes snorkellers beneath the waves to glimpse furry-hatted plumose anemone, red-eyed velvet swimming crabs and purpley-pink maerl, a type of hard algae.

Worth a stop is the vibrant **Loch Torridon Community Centre**, home to a cafe and gallery. Check its events calendar: live music, storytelling nights, movie screenings and craft markets are often on the agenda.

Around 9 km (5.5 miles) to the west of Torridon, a single-track road leads to the **Bealach na Gaoithe Viewpoint**. It might be a dead-end road, but the trip is still very much worthwhile: from here, views across the mountain-encircled Loch Torridon and towards the rugged Applecross Peninsula unspool before you.

Torridon Outdoors
W thetorridon.com/torridon-outdoors

Torridon Snorkel Trail
W scottishwildlifetrust.org.uk/things-to-do/snorkel-trails

Loch Torridon Community Centre
///photocopy.sending.heap ⌂ 18 km (11 miles) west of Kinlochewe, along single-track road in Torridon Village P On-site ⊙ Hours vary, check website W lochtorridoncentre.co.uk

Bealach na Gaoithe Viewpoint
///elects.enchanted.issues P 9 km (5.5 miles) from Torridon; unsignposted on the east side of the road

Left The small village of Torridon, with hulking mountains rising behind it

99 Shieldaig

Founded in the early 1800s, this tranquil seaside village has been both a training ground for Royal Navy sailors preparing to battle Napoleon and a bustling fishing hub (its name comes from the Old Norse *"sild-vik"*, meaning "herring bay"). Today, it's a welcome stop for many visitors on the North Coast 500, thanks to a handful of great places to eat. Not that it ever feels too busy – apart from the first weekend in August, that is, when the Shieldaig Fete and Coastal Rowing Regatta puts on a show.

The village's pretty location – tucked away on the shore of Loch Shieldaig – is best appreciated on a walk north along the An Aird peninsula. There are superb views back towards the village, as well as the chance to see wildlife like herons and otters. There's also excellent sea kayaking here, including out to the Caledonian pine-covered Shieldaig Island, a scenic spot managed by the NTS; according to local lore, the trees here were planted to provide a way for fishers to dry their nets. Check out **Shieldaig Outdoor Adventures** for kayaking and canoeing trips.

Shieldaig Outdoor Adventures
W shieldaigadventures.com

100 Applecross Sands

///lawns.blank.clerics P 7 km (4.5 miles) from Applecross; unsignposted on the west side of the road

From Shieldaig, the road presents more of a challenge, twisting and turning along the edge of the remote Applecross

Roughly 13 km (8 miles) from Shieldaig, reached along the peninsula's wiggling roads, is **Applecross Smokehouse** (///applause. tastier.footpath; applecrosssmokehouse.co.uk). This unassuming spot is run by Derrick MacIver, who once fished the surrounding coast for shellfish, and his wife Lorna, with all of the smoking happening on-site in a purpose-built shed, found at the end of their garden. There's a little shop next door, too, where the fish is sold: choose from hot-smoked or cold-smoked options, both of which are delicious. Before you leave, cast your eye around the well-kept garden; as Derrick and Lorna will probably tell you, it's a regular haunt for a family of pine martens.

Peninsula. It might be a tiring route to navigate, but it also serves up a big dose of beautiful coastal scenery as it goes, with epic views across Loch Torridon and the surrounding mountains, as well as over the sea to the rugged isles of Rona, Raasay and Skye.

Eventually, on the western side of the peninsula, this beautiful beach comes into view. Its far northern end is a submarine testing station, owned by the Ministry of Defence, but the rest of the beach is open to the public. Come low tide, its golden sands are streaked with pockets of water, making it a great place for a paddle, while above the beach stands a 9,500-year-old Mesolithic rock shelter.

From here, a path leads to the hamlet of Applecross, roughly 7 km (4.5 miles) away. Expect more stunning views, this time out towards the Raasay and Skye.

Clockwise from top left Derrick, owner of Applecross Smokehouse; the shop at the end of the garden; Derrick cutting a slice of salmon to smoke; the sign at the front of the house

⑩ Applecross

This loose handful of houses along Shore Street is often referred to as Applecross by visitors. But say that to a long-standing local and you'll be quickly corrected: Applecross is the peninsula itself. Whatever its name, this little hamlet, fringing a U-shaped bay, is the peninsula's main settlement, with scattered accommodation, public toilets, a top-notch inn and even a petrol station. Two pleasant short walks start in the village. A 3.5-km (2.25-mile) circuit passes by an Iron Age broch and a reconstructed roundhouse, while a slightly longer 4-km (2.5-mile) trail passes woodland and a river, before skirting the edge of the settlement's shingle beach. See WalkHighlands *(p15)* for more information.

Just north is the **Applecross Heritage Centre**. This locally run museum recounts the area's history, including the arrival of Christianity, with a particularly good selection of 19th-century artifacts. A highlight is a rare 8th-century carved cross slab – the only example of its kind in the Highlands – that beautifully blends Pictish and Irish art forms.

The hamlet is also home to **Applecross Walled Garden**. Built during the Victorian era as a vegetable garden for nearby Applecross House, it's now a riot of colour come spring and summer thanks to its beautiful selection of flowers, including

lavender, tulips and roses. Vegetables are still grown, mind you, and often used in the excellent on-site cafe (the seafood is all locally sourced, too). If you're visiting on a Sunday, stick around for live music from local bands.

Applecross Heritage Centre

///habit.animate.schematic 🏠 Unsignposted, on east side of single-track road as you come into Applecross village 🅿 On-site 🕒 Apr–Oct: noon–4pm daily 🅦 applecrossheritage.org.uk

Applecross Walled Garden

///zipped.stunts.relishing 🏠 Signposted off single-track road through Applecross village 🅿 On-site 🕒 Hours vary, check website 🅦 applecrossgarden.co.uk

Applecross might be small, but it's home to one of the best pubs on the route: the **Applecross Inn** (*///unscathed.subject.worm; applecrossinn.co.uk*). Perched on the edge of the bay, this whitewashed building is a great place for a nightcap, with plenty of Scottish gins and whiskies on the menu, plus beers courtesy of the village's very own Applecross Brewing Co. Depending on the weather, you can cosy up in the wood-panelled bar or take a seat outside to watch the sun set over the bay.

Left Fruit and vegetable patches in Applecross Walled Garden, watched over by a rather dapper scarecrow

102 Bealach na Bà

Arguably the most impressive stretch of road on the North Coast 500, this alpine-style mountain pass wriggles its way up from sea level at Applecross village, reaching a height of 626 m (2,053 ft), before plunging back down to tiny Tornapress at the end of Loch Kishorn. The road itself was constructed in 1822, but local people have been using the route for around 2,000 years. Its name comes from the drovers who once herded their cattle across it – Bealach na Bà is Gaelic for "Pass of the Cattle".

The route isn't for the faint of heart. It takes in blind bends, sheer drops, and steep ascents and descents – up to 20 per cent in some places. And that's not even mentioning the series of incredibly tight hairpin turns, including one that's not-so-reassuringly known as the "devil's elbow". High season also brings a high volume of traffic; while there are a good number of passing places along the way, you'll still nevertheless need to keep your wits about you.

Suffice to say, this isn't a road that should be taken by inexperienced or nervous drivers, or by those with long vehicles or caravans. That's not just for visitors' safety, either; the road is a lifeline route for local people, providing crucial access to emergency services. Luckily, there's a more direct – and flatter – route from Shieldaig to Tornapress if it's not for you.

With all that being said, some of the most spectacular views on the route await drivers who do tackle the road. From the top, rugged mountain landscapes unfurl all around, stretching across the twinkling sea towards the isles of Skye, Rona and the Outer Hebrides; at sunset, their outlines reach towards the horizon in graduated shades of blue.

Near the foot of the Bealach na Bà is **Kishorn Seafood Bar** (////partner. duplicity.apart; kishornseafoodbar.co.uk). This powder-blue wooden cabin sits just off the A896 and is famous for its fresh-from-the-ocean dishes, including sumptuous seafood platters and tasty fish pies. Thanks to the west coast's bounty of seafood, most of the ingredients used are sourced locally, including prawns from Loch Torridon and oysters from Skye.

Clockwise from top left Looking down the Bealach towards Applecross; a lochan at the top of the pass; the switchbacks near the summit on the Tornapress side

Clockwise from top left Vicky holding a handmade item; inside the welcoming Balnacra Pottery; a selection of mugs made by Vicky; the cheerful exterior of the pottery

⟨103⟩ Lochcarron

The last west coast village on the route, Lochcarron is a daisy chain of whitewashed houses strung along the shores of Loch Carron. It's a handy spot to pick up any final supplies, with a supermarket and petrol station, and has some cute cafes and pubs. Pay a visit to the **Smithy Community Hub,** too, a community-run venue home to an eclectic group of creators and makers. Here, you'll find the store of the community's very own Lochcarron Weavers, selling a vast array of tartans (there are over 700 styles), as well as Balnacra Pottery. Housed in a 19th-century smithy and forge, this welcoming pottery is run by Vicky Stonebridge, who sells an array of handcrafted items, from pretty glazed bowls to smoke-fired vases made using ancient Pictish techniques. Keep an eye out for pottery classes here, too.

While other sights are thin on the ground, the village does make a great base for exploring the surrounding area. Around 6.5 km (4 miles) from Lochcarron lie the eerie ruins of 15th-century Strome Castle, while further south in Plockton sits the family-run **Lilias's Garden,** known for its rhododendrons, waterfalls and wildflower meadows, plus stunning views over lochs Carron and Kishorn. Also close by is the ever-colourful Attadale Gardens *(p186)*.

There are walks aplenty around Lochcarron, too. Looking for something gentle? The 2-km (1.25-mile) walk through pretty Strome Wood should do the trick. If a mountain hike is on the cards, the ascent up the Maol Chean-dearg Munro is a great option; its Gaelic name means

"bald red head" thanks to its summit of red sandstone. See WalkHighlands *(p15)*, as always, for more information. Water babies won't feel left out, either, with **Sea Kayak Plockton** taking tours out on Loch Carron.

Smithy Community Hub
///cookies.work.equivocal 🏠 Ribhuachan, Strathcarron; signposted off the A896 🅿 On-site 🕐 Hours vary, check websites 🔳 Lochcarron Weavers: lochcarron. co.uk; Balnacra Pottery: balnacra.com

Lilias's Garden
///glossed.envy.spots 🏠 Rudha Mor, Plockton, 30 km (20 miles) southwest of Lochcarron 🅿 Public parking south end of Harbour Street, then 10-minute walk 🕐 Hours vary, check website 🔳 rudhamorplockton.co.uk 💰 Donation

Sea Kayak Plockton
🔳 seakayakplockton.co.uk

From Lochcarron, the A890 winds alongside the coast and across hills to reach the Isle of Skye. This famed island is worth a whole trip in its own right, although it's possible to scoop up some of the highlights over a long weekend. While the island is best known for its otherworldly landscapes, including the soaring Cullins and the rocky ramparts of the Quairing, there's plenty more to explore, from remote Neist Lighthouse to seaside Portree, the island's main town.

⑩④ Attadale Gardens

///hexes.hails.backhand 🏠 I I km (7 miles) southeast of Lochcarron; signposted off the A890 🅿 On-site ⏰ End Mar–Oct: 10am–5pm daily 🔲 attadalegardens. com 🐾 🎧 Audio tour

Variety is the name of the game at this award-winning garden, across the water from Lochcarron *(p184)*, with views over to Skye. As well as rhododendron-dotted woodland, there's a whole host of gardens, including a tranquil Japanese garden, home to dwarf conifers and Japanese maples, a pretty water garden with a Monet-style lily pond and a sunken garden brimming with ferns.

Established during the Victorian period, Attadale's gardens were extensively redeveloped in the later 20th century by Nicky Macphenson, an artist, and her husband Ewen. Nicky's artistic touch is found throughout the gardens, both in the beautiful groupings of plants and the sculptures – produced by both local and international artists – strewn across the grounds. Keep an eye out for those depicting local wildlife, including a heron and an otter.

⑩⑤ Ben Wyvis

///headboard.clean.promises 🅿 6.5 km (4 miles) northeast of Garve; signposted off the A835

After the drama of the west coast, the flatter land and straighter roads leading to Inverness can feel a bit underwhelming. But it's not quite over yet. As the route snakes towards the village of Garve, the monumental form of Ben Wyvis appears like a sleeping leviathan on the horizon.

This flat-ridged mountain can be climbed via a relatively straightforward trail, although there is a tough section up a stone staircase to the top of An Cabar; see WalkHighlands *(p15)* for more information. The mountain itself is relatively isolated from any peers, meaning the views from the summit on a clear day stretch for miles, including east to the Fannich range and south to the Cairngorm massif.

⑩⑥ Rogie Falls

///stickler.engrossed.permit 🅿 6.5 km (4 miles) southeast of Garve; signposted off the A835 🔲 forestryandland.gov.scot

As the route passes Loch Garve, it plunges into thick forest, within which sits this eye-catching waterfall. It's just a short walk from the car park to reach these treacle-coloured falls, which tumble down between moss-and-lichen-covered rocks. The best views are from the suspension bridge strung across the aptly named Black Water river; here, in August and September, wild salmon make the leap upstream.

There are some lovely walks nearby, including the Riverside Trail, which follows the flow of the river to Raven's Crag, another viewpoint, before dipping into woodland, the forest floor carpeted with blaeberry bushes and heather. On the other side of the river, trails snake further into the woodland – see WalkHighlands *(p15)* for more information.

⑩ Strathpeffer

A short distance off the North Coast 500, this old spa town is the last stop before Inverness. Lying huddled among wooded hills, it was a buzzing spot during the Victorian era, with people coming from as far as London to "take the waters". While much quieter today, it still retains a refined air thanks to its elegant architecture.

A handful of sights nod to its past, including the elegant **Strathpeffer Pavilion**. It was constructed in the late 19th century as an entertainment venue for visitors, with the likes of Emmeline Pankhurst and Ernest Shackleton coming to deliver lectures. Today, it's a community-owned events venue, hosting everything from craft fairs to live music. Nearby is one of the original pump rooms; it once held exhibits on the area's spa history, but is currently closed for development.

Opposite the pavilion is the main square, which has an energetic vibe during summer, with tables from local cafes spilling out onto the streets and live music performed in the bandstand. Not far from here is the **Eagle Stone**, a carved Pictish symbol stone, while a little further on lies the old railway station, today home to an excellent cafe, cute shop and the homespun yet absorbing **Highland Museum of Childhood**.

There are several good walking trails in the area (see WalkHighlands, *p15*), with an accessible trail alongside the Black Water river in nearby Contin woodlands. From here, it's around 30 km (20 miles) to Inverness *(p20)*, whose welcoming bars and restaurants are a great place to celebrate the end of your North Coast 500 adventure.

Strathpeffer Pavilion
///dugouts.studs.code ⌂ The Square
🅿 On-site ⏰ Hours for events vary, check website
🅦 highlifehighland.com/strathpefferpavilion

Eagle Stone
///steady.towns.installs ⌂ Signposted off the A834, a 5-minute walk from The Square 🅿 The Square

Highland Museum of Childhood
///deck.loopholes.sporting ⌂ The Old Station, signposted off the A834 🅿 On-site
⏰ 10am–3pm Tue–Sat (from 11.30am Sat)
🅦 highlandmuseumofchildhood.org.uk ⤢

In the centre of Strathpeffer, the **Deli In The Square** (////boomers.goofy.harshest; deliinthesquare.co.uk) covers all the bases, from coffee and cake in the morning to pizza and beer in the evening, And, as its name suggests, there's a deli on-site, too.

After something sweet? Try the **Station Cafe** (07498 527022; ///waddle.reprints.offer) in Strathpeffer's old railway station. There's always plenty of baking on offer, with a good range of vegan and gluten-free options. Try the sumptuous chocolate and caramel cake or go for a good old-fashioned scone, doused in jam and cream.

Housed in a light and bright glasshouse, **Unwined Cafe** (////dose.lamplight.transfers; 07506 909678) has a surprisingly Mediterranean vibe, especially in summer, when its tables and chairs spill outside. The menu is excellent and ever-changing, and can cover everything from snackable small plates to hearty roast dinners.

Index

Author

Rachel Laidler is an editor and writer at the award-winning DK Travel. On her previous adventures she's hiked in Nepal's Himalayas, solo-tripped through Italy by train and raised calves on a dairy farm in New Zealand. After a couple of years in Inverness, she's now Edinburgh-based, but still loves nothing more than heading north to explore the Scottish Highlands.

Photographer

Daniel Alford is a travel photographer who loves capturing both beautiful landscapes and intimate human stories with his camera. His work has taken him from the Tian Shan mountains of Kyrgyzstan (where he searched for snow leopards) to the rugged fjords of Greenland. Daniel regularly works with clients such as National Geographic, Barbour and Netflix. See more of his work at danielalford.co.uk.

Picture Credits

The publisher would like to thank the following for their kind permission to reproduce their photographs:

(Key: a-above; b-below/bottom; c-centre; f-far; l-left; r-right; t-top)

Alamy Stock Photo: Tony Banks 62b; Alan Keith Beastall 101; CMH.Images 108–109; Gary Cook 172bl; Paul Glendell 62t; Jan Holm 34–35; George Maciver 65; Simon Turner 176; Tursiops Photography 40t.
Dreamstime.com: Eddie Cloud 149.
Getty Images / iStock: Esra Sen Kula All-Pages (Icons).
Shutterstock.com: Guillaume Angleraud 170–171.

Cover images: *Front:* **Getty Images:** Chris J / 500px l; **Getty Images / iStock:** Esra Sen Kula r (Icons).

The rate at which the world is changing is constantly keeping the DK Travel team on our toes. While we've worked hard to ensure this book is accurate and up-to-date, things can change in an instant. Road conditions can worsen, petrol stations can close and weather can impact your travel plans. Road closures often occur in winter months, so it's important to check ahead before embarking on your road trip. The publisher cannot accept responsibility for any consequences arising from the use of this book. If you notice we've got something wrong, we want to hear about it. Please get in touch at travelguides@dk.com

Project Editor Rachel Laidler
Senior Designer Laura O'Brien
Designer James Boast
Proofreader Kathryn Glendenning
Indexer Helen Peters
Jacket Designers Gemma Doyle, Laura O'Brien, Cristina Antequera
Publishing Assistant Simona Velikova
Senior Cartographic Editor James Macdonald
Production Editor David Almond
Production Controller Kariss Ainsworth
Managing Art Editor Gemma Doyle
Editorial Director Hollie Teague
Art Director Maxine Pedliham
Publishing Director Georgina Dee

First edition 2025

Published in Great Britain by Dorling Kindersley Limited in association with North Coast 500 Ltd, 20 Vauxhall Bridge Road, London SW1V 2SA

The authorised representative in the EEA is Dorling Kindersley Verlag GmbH. Arnulfstr. 124, 80636 Munich, Germany

Published in the United States by DK Publishing in association with North Coast 500 Ltd, 1745 Broadway, 20th Floor, New York, NY 10019, USA

Copyright © 2025 Dorling Kindersley Limited
A Penguin Random House Company

NC500™ and North Coast 500™ are trademarks of North Coast 500 Limited and may be registered in some countries

25 26 27 28 10 9 8 7 6 5 4 3 2 1

A CIP catalog record for this book is available from the British Library.

A catalog record for this book is available from the Library of Congress.

ISSN: 1542 1554
ISBN: 978 0 2417 3319 6

Printed and bound in China.

www.dk.com

MIX
Paper | Supporting responsible forestry
FSC™ C018179

This book was made with Forest Stewardship Council™ certified paper – one small step in DK's commitment to a sustainable future. **Learn more at www.dk.com/uk/information/sustainability**